COMPETITIVE ADVANTAGE IN THE CONTRACTING BUSINESS

BUSINESS ISSUES, COMPETITION AND ENTREPRENEURSHIP SERIES

BUSINESS ISSUES, COMPETITION AND ENTREPRENEURSHIP SERIES

COMPETITIVE ADVANTAGE IN THE CONTRACTING BUSINESS

LOW SUI PHENG, FAISAL MANZOOR ARAIN

AND

LIM TING TING

Nova Science Publishers, Inc.
New York

For permission to use material from this book please contact us:
Telephone 631-231-7269; Fax 631-231-8175
Web Site: http://www.novapublishers.com

NOTICE TO THE READER

The Publisher has taken reasonable care in the preparation of this book, but makes no expressed or implied warranty of any kind and assumes no responsibility for any errors or omissions. No liability is assumed for incidental or consequential damages in connection with or arising out of information contained in this book. The Publisher shall not be liable for any special, consequential, or exemplary damages resulting, in whole or in part, from the readers' use of, or reliance upon, this material.

Independent verification should be sought for any data, advice or recommendations contained in this book. In addition, no responsibility is assumed by the publisher for any injury and/or damage to persons or property arising from any methods, products, instructions, ideas or otherwise contained in this publication.

This publication is designed to provide accurate and authoritative information with regard to the subject matter covered herein. It is sold with the clear understanding that the Publisher is not engaged in rendering legal or any other professional services. If legal or any other expert assistance is required, the services of a competent person should be sought. FROM A DECLARATION OF PARTICIPANTS JOINTLY ADOPTED BY A COMMITTEE OF THE AMERICAN BAR ASSOCIATION AND A COMMITTEE OF PUBLISHERS.

LIBRARY OF CONGRESS CATALOGING-IN-PUBLICATION DATA

Low, Sui Pheng.
  Competitive advantage in the contracting business / Low Sui Pheng, Faisal Manzoor Arain, Lim Ting Ting.
     p. cm.
  Includes bibliographical references and index.
  ISBN 978-1-60876-800-4 (hardcover)
  1. Construction industry--Technological innovations--Case studies. 2. Competition--Case studies. I. Arain, Faisal Manzoor. II. Ting, Lim Ting. III. Title.
  HD9715.A2L668 2009
  624.068'4--dc22   2009048940

Published by Nova Science Publishers, Inc. ✦ *New York*

CONTENTS

PREFACE

The construction industry can be a complex and extremely competitive industry. There are many stakeholders, both internal and external, who contribute not only to the complexity and competition but also to some degree, fragmentation in the industry. All this makes the business of contracting even more daunting and challenging for some if not all firms in the construction industry. The more progressive construction firms therefore constantly seek to improve their business acumen vis-à-vis their competitors.

All construction firms have a strategy, explicit or implicit. The construction industry today is faced with an increasingly turbulent operating environment that demands a deeper examination of the operations and activities of construction firms. To perform well in the marketplace, construction firms need to examine all the available sources of competitive advantage, demonstrate how all of these advantages can be connected to specific activities within the business and the manner in which these integrate with one another within their own value chains as well as those of their clients'.

It is with this context in mind that we discuss and validate the three generic business strategies popularized by Michael Porter to examine if all three strategies are mutually exclusive or supportive. We also ascertain the underlying sources of competitive advantage of construction firms and examine the importance of technology in contributing to the competitive advantage of construction firms. We note a myriad of different strategies that can be used by construction firms, including the hybrid strategy which Michael Porter regards it to be undesirable, seeing it as being "stuck in the middle". Nevertheless, we recommend that regardless of what these competitive strategies are, construction firms should leverage on their strong points to improve their implementation abilities.

Our study of the competitive advantage of construction firms in Singapore show that a majority of these firms, in the cost advantage segment, have invested the least in technology as compared to those in the differentiating and hybrid segments. The reluctance of the construction firms towards adopting and implementing technology came about primarily through their lack of capital and the impractical applications of a "one size fits all" technology across all their projects. On the other hand, we also found that technology does have an overwhelming impact in terms of enhancing a firm's performance against their competitors. Most construction firms, in all the strategic segments, have expressed the importance of entering into partnerships to build rapport with the property developers, suppliers and subcontractors. This is to establish good working relationships and ensure repeat orders from their clients.

We are well aware that the business strategies adopted by construction firms may take on a different approach depending on the economic situation at a specific point in time. Construction firms should be able to find their competitive advantage in the business of contracting if they are able to relate their operations with the findings which we have presented in this book.

Chapter 1

INTRODUCTION

BUSINESS STRATEGIES IN POSITIVE ENVIRONMENT

Like all other business entities, construction firms function in a marketplace that can show seasonally positive and adverse operating environments. A study of how construction firms fared in a positive business environment was undertaken by Low (1992) who also highlighted the strategies adopted by construction firms to help them prepare for and ensure their long-term survival when the building industry is still performing well. These strategies as planned ahead by construction firms in a positive business environment then prevalent in 1992 in Singapore, in anticipation of a slowdown in construction activities included the following.

Consolidation

Many construction firms see consolidation as an important strategy to counter a slump in the building industry. To consolidate, firms would need to monitor their construction costs and overheads carefully. Constant managerial improvement is needed to control wastages and costs in the business. One method commonly mentioned by construction firms relates to the use of information technology to help expedite managerial efficacy (Low, 1992).

Construction firms also advocated discarding the "wait and see" attitude atypical of many traditional, family-run businesses in Asia. The need to plan ahead carefully was instead stressed by construction firms, although this may seem possible only for the larger corporations and public listed companies where funds for the betterment of managerial expertise are available more readily. It is, however, heartening to note that construction firms are more inclined to move towards this direction for them to remain and become more competitive. Construction firms would fundamentally need to adopt good management structures and be financially sound to see their businesses through any impending slump in the building industry (Low, 1992).

Upgrading

Many construction firms have heeded the advice to upgrade their productivity and technological base when the building industry is still performing well. In this context, responses to the call for increased productivity, better site management, upgrading information technology, continuing professional development of staff and the adoption of new technology such as prefabrication have been positive (Low, 1992). Many construction firms have adopted stricter control measures to improve quality standards and employed more qualified building professionals and skilled workers to constantly improve site and quality management.

Construction firms are also adopting a more professional approach to building by recruiting and training staff in design-build contracts as well as constructability in anticipation of a surge in demand in these areas (Low, 1992). In addition, construction firms have noted that the development of expertise in these areas would help them to expand their operations overseas. Continuous improvement and the formulation of new methods for managing projects through the employment of competent management staff and professionals have also received attention.

Joint ventures present yet another avenue for construction firms to upgrade themselves in areas which they would not possibly have undertaken on their own. However, construction firms who have had experience with joint ventures recommended that a more established relationship with joint venture partners should be encouraged in the long run.

The misconception of a moratorium on investments in plant and equipment as a precaution is generally absent among construction firms (Low, 1992). Construction firms will not hesitate to invest in basic plant and equipment if these are necessary for them to increase their productivity and so long as these plant and equipment prove to be viable economically relative to the amount and size of their building projects. However, construction firms do not favor the adoption of complex automation or the purchase of capital intensive labor-saving machineries. This is because of a fear that the purchase of these costly machineries may not fully justify the capital outlay as a result of the nature of the building industry where future projects and continuity of work cannot be guaranteed. Consequently, the risks associated with investments in these costly machineries will be higher.

Procurement

Construction firms frequently review and plan their backlog of projects to minimize idling resources at any one time. Nevertheless, construction firms should not over-stretch their resources unnecessarily by securing too many jobs at one time. Timing of jobs is therefore important for construction firms.

Although construction firms may have been fortunate to secure sufficient jobs to help tide them over the recession in the mid-1980s in Singapore, this stop-gap measure will need to be evaluated cautiously by construction firms today (Low, 1992). The ability to bridge over bad times is dependent on the firm's ability, confidence and success rate in tendering. A high success rate can be elusive today because of the keen competition faced by many more construction firms. When sizeable building projects are lacking in the marketplace, some larger construction firms would resort to securing smaller jobs to help tide them over difficult times. The larger construction firms, however, face a disadvantage when competing for small jobs with the smaller construction firms. This is because the latter generally operate with lower overheads and are therefore better able to submit more competitive bids (Low, 1992).

Diversification

Diversification is fast becoming an increasing popular strategy among construction firms. It would be strategic to diversify only into industries which are performing well. Hence, there is a constant need to source for these opportunities both within and outside the construction arena. Construction firms have diversified into property development, retrofitting works and general trading in descending order of priority. Construction firms should, however, only expand into areas which they are familiar with or where the necessary experience and expertise have already been acquired; for example, through a take-over bid of an established firm in that business segment. To do otherwise may actually cause more harm than good because a new business venture takes, on average, about two years to establish itself and become profitable. This may further strain the financial position of the construction firm instead of helping to improve its bottom line. In addition, industries which are profitable would also tend to attract more competition in the market.

If the financial position of a construction firm permits, it should expand overseas to countries with robust construction industries. However, the firm should continue to retain its presence in the domestic market to maintain its established track record for it to move upstream in the building industry (Low, 1992).

The study completed by Low (1992) when the building industry was performing well showed that different diversification strategies were then in vouch. These are described below.

Sectoral Diversification in the Building Industry

Construction firms appear to be against the idea of relying only on a single client for jobs either in the public sector or the private sector. Specialization in a particular sector is also discouraged. Construction firms should therefore be flexible enough and be prepared to switch between sectors to where jobs are available.

Diversification into Specialized Construction Related Activities

These include activities such as retrofitting works in the public sector which construction firms may view as a pump-priming strategy adopted by the government to cushion the impact of any imminent slow-down in the building industry. It will be opportune for construction firms to acquire the relevant know-how during a building boom to expand into this sector.

Diversification into Property Development

Construction firms who are financially sound or who have reaped profits during the boom times have diversified into property development. Their commitments to building up their land banks can help to facilitate possible diversification into property development during a slump when in-house development works may be initiated as a stop-gap measure to help tide them over the bad times.

Diversification into Overseas Markets

Construction firms have recognized the need to export their services overseas, especially when large scale building projects are dwindling in a small domestic market. The intense competition faced by the larger construction firms from the smaller construction firms when both tender for small building projects is another reason why the former are eager to venture abroad. Nonetheless, although overseas markets may appear attractive, there are also attendant hurdles and difficulties associated with making a foray abroad. In penetrating foreign markets, the capital outlay needed to set up overseas offices and in persuading local staff to be stationed abroad for extended period of time are important considerations.

Diversification into other Non-construction Related Activities

These include activities such as trading, agency works and franchises, etc. However, construction firms without the necessary experience in these areas should be prudent when contemplating diversification into non-construction related activities. They should instead first consider exploring diversification into activities which are construction-related. Nevertheless, a knowledge and insight of other non-construction related activities should be gathered to prepare them to diversify into these activities when the opportunity arises in the future.

STRATEGIC BEHAVIOR IN ADVERSE ENVIRONMENT

The business strategies adopted by construction firms in a positive business environment were described above (Low, 1992). This section explains the corresponding strategic behavior of construction firms when they operate in an adverse business environment such as that presented by the Asian financial crisis (Low and Lim, 1999). The financial crisis in Asia first started in July 1997 in Thailand following the devaluation of the Thai Baht. This crisis soon spilled over to other neighboring Asian countries, affecting in the process Indonesia and Malaysia and further afield to Hong Kong and South Korea where currencies were devalued drastically overnight. The economic downturn, which followed the financial crisis in Asia, has also affected countries in other parts of the world, including Latin America and Europe.

Like other economic sectors, the construction industry has also not been spared from the economic crisis. However, unlike other economic sectors such as the manufacturing industry where demand may be undermined almost immediately, this is not usually the case in the construction industry, which enjoys two distinct advantages (Low, 1992). Firstly, the long gestation in building projects mean that contracts, which were awarded in 1997, will only be completed two to three years later. The gestation in construction is primarily dependent on the size and complexity of the building project. The larger and more complex the project is, the longer its gestation. This means that the projects won by a contractor in 1997 may actually help to tide the company over the next two or three years. Nevertheless, this scenario assumes that the financial crisis has not affected the liquidity of the developer-owner who can still finance the project through to completion. Secondly, because of the forward and backward linkages, which the construction industry has with other economic sectors, the construction industry is often used as a stimulus by the government to pump-prime the economy. This is achieved by bringing forward major infrastructure projects and other public sector building projects. Apart from pump-priming the economy, the Treasury also stands to gain from the lower bid prices for public sector projects as competition becomes more intense among the job-hungry construction firms.

An economic downturn normally motivates private corporations to undertake unusual steps to protect their assets from continued decline (King and Cushman, 1997). Strategies should, at least until the crisis is over, generally avoid any fundamental change in character of a business as well as major changes in the business interface with customers which are likely to confuse them such as changes in sales personnel and distribution channels (Prescott, 1982). The following broad strategies should be considered to better understand how firms behave in an economic downturn:

1. Restructuring
2. Shrink selectively
3. Marketing
4. Cost cutting
5. Long-term strategies
6. Other measures.

These strategic responses to an economic downturn are discussed below.

Restructuring

Restructuring is the process of transferring production from an expensive site to a cheaper one. It may involve the transfer of activities from a developed to developing country or from high to low wage countries (Cordova and Dror, 1984) as in the case of Japanese firms moving their operations overseas (King and Cushman, 1997). Townsend (1983) observed that in the recession in the United Kingdom in the 1980s, virtually all major corporations at some point in time restructured their activities in the face of over-capacity and high costs.

Process restructuring covers marketing, product development, production, purchasing, finance and after-sales service (Kozminski, 1997). Its main objective is to bring the company to an acceptable minimum level of performance. Production restructuring, for example, leads to improvement in quality, elimination of waste and reduction of the production cycle. Cost improvement can be achieved through out-sourcing and buying directly from the producer. There is evidence to suggest that the larger firms are out-sourcing some of their activities to specialist firms (Tingle, 1994). The selection of local talents, with some background in management and providing them with training, forms part of functional restructuring. Laying off redundant staff and intensive training in functional skills can help to enable successful functional restructuring only if coupled with basic structural design to provide for the elimination of most of the hierarchical layers of the old structure. Employees are encouraged to acquire new skills and to further develop skills and capabilities that they already possessed (Kozminski, 1997). Workers who are affected by technological changes should be entitled to full retraining during office hours at the employer's expense (Cordova and Dror, 1984).

Down-sizing may occur by reducing workload as well as eliminating functions, hierarchical layers or units and by streamlining activities. Down-sizing has helped companies in Japan and the United States to lower overheads, speeds up response time, eliminates red tape/bottlenecks and increases productivity (King and Cushman, 1997). The shedding of staff associated with restructuring may happen together with redundancies caused by divestments. Consequently, some form of reorganization of industrial practices, the introduction of new methods of managerial control and the substitution of labor by more up-to-date equipment may need to be instituted (Danson, 1986). Many companies in the United States were once lean and mean as a result of the restructuring exercise undertaken in the 1980s. Measures such as huge layoffs, reduced executive travel and lower entertainment budget are, however, less likely to provide room for maneuver (Palmer, 1991). The following scenarios should be considered in restructuring:

1. Changing top management when transiting from one restructuring phase to another (Kozminski, 1997; Whiltington, 1989).
2. Adding new people (with new skills) to mange teams filled by individuals outside the organization, particularly if the organization has been growing rapidly before the crisis (Kozminski, 1997; Slatter, 1992).
3. Constant head-hunting, training and investments in human capital remain the essence of building up managerial competence (Kozminski, 1997).

4. Educate management and labor about the new reality brought about by the crisis (Nueno, 1993).
5. Management attitude must be changed permanently (Shilling, 1988).

Shrink Selectively

The principal product-market strategies, which can be employed to re-position a company's business as part of the strategy to shrink selectively, include the following:

1. Focus on specific product-market segments (Slatter, 1992; Shilling, 1988; Whiltington, 1989; Palmer, 1991; Morine, 1980; Prescott, 1982) which provide a profitable core of higher margin sales (Palmer, 1991; Prescott, 1982) and require least working capital to support them (Prescott, 1982).
2. Withdraw from unprofitable market segments (Slatter, 1992; Whiltington, 1989; Palmer, 1991) to a point where the firm is operating from a more secure base of lower volume but higher margin business (Palmer, 1991).
3. Sale of investments to get funds with higher rates of return in the principal activities of the business (Morine, 1980).
4. Contract the business to one entity which will generally lower the level of fixed costs and capital employed (Prescott, 1982).
5. Introduce value added (Slatter, 1992) or develop proprietary products (Shilling, 1988).
6. Shift position in the value-adding chain (Slatter, 1992).
7. Cutbacks are sometimes necessary if much of the recently acquired business is low margin business and the firm faces critical cash-flow problems (Palmer, 1991).

Marketing

An economic downturn, in which there is a decline in consumer spending power, offers opportunities for profitable sales in so far as improved products are concerned (Committee for Economic Development, 1954). Marketing is therefore a more desirable alternative to increase volume instead of cutting profit margins or continually discounting prices (Morine, 1980). Palmer (1991) argued that companies wishing to thrive in an economic downturn should not be cutting back on marketing and product development but should instead increase the budget for marketing activities. In this context, market improvement activities have actually helped firms to survive in post-communist Central and Eastern European countries during their recessions (Kozminski, 1997).

As part of its marketing function, the firm will need to keep in constant touch with its existing client base, introduce quick adjustments to its portfolio, and re-focus on client's needs for financing, promotion, quality and design (Palmer, 1991). Attention should also be paid to delivery, time-saving product features, reliable after-sales service and back-up, aesthetic features of the product, a unique, functional and convenient feature of the product and so on (Palmer, 1991; Morine 1980). Marketing policies will need to be redefined in line with customer shifts for more value-adding products/services at lower prices (Slatter, 1992).

Cost Cutting

In most businesses, cost reduction is a faster method to achieve greater profits than increasing sales volume. In addition, cost reduction measures do not usually invoke a response from competitors (Morine, 1980). Cost cutting also helps to tackle a cash-flow crisis within a business (Slatter, 1992). Hence, the adoption of typical cost cutting measures to minimize wastage and unnecessary expenditure constitutes an important survival tactic for a business in a downturn (Low, 1992; Shilling, 1988; Whiltington, 1989). The typical cost cutting measures include the following:

1. Working hours and wages – to be reduced as well as cuts in bonuses (Chen, 1985).
2. Human resource – switching from seniority-based promotion and pay system to one that is based on ability and merit; retrenchment of unproductive employees; compulsory upgrading of skills and knowledge by older workers and so on (Cordova and Dror, 1984).
3. Productivity – profit sharing creates an incentive for employees to enhance productivity (Shilling, 1988).
4. Bigger orders and lower bids – rewarding suppliers who meet quality standards with bigger orders help to achieve lower bids (Shilling, 1988).
5. Competitive bidding – where subcontractors are selected through competitive bidding rather than through negotiation (Palmer, 1991).

6. Time – management of time to include the handling of paperwork only once, cutting back on report writing and holding fewer meetings to save time (Nueno, 1993).

7. Overheads – immediate and drastic overheads cost reduction forms part of the turn-around strategy, including turning off unnecessary lights, making telephone calls at off-peak hours and reducing unnecessary travel (Slatter, 1992).

8. Rationalizing personnel – the reduction of employment involves the rationalization of productive capacity and product lines (Danson, 1986; Townsend, 1983). Only the core personnel are retained and utilized fully to minimize overheads. Additional staff can then be employed on a project basis (Low, 1992).

9. Rely on inexperienced staff – where young and inexperienced employees are employed to take on a larger scope of work, including that of older employees who have been made redundant (Prescott, 1982).

10. Stock control – minimize the level of unproductive stocks that are held as this lowers interest charges as well as costs of warehousing and materials handling (Prescott, 1982; Palmer, 1991).

Long-term Strategies

A business is only as viable as its future. All businesses therefore need long-term plans and strategies. The following list of strategies should be considered by all businesses for their long-term planning in an economic downturn:

1. Availability of funds – cultivate relationships with potential sources of funds, keeping them abreast of the company's performance and plans so that when their resources are needed, there is an on-going understanding of the prevailing situation and a willingness to help (Shilling, 1988; Palmer, 1991).

2. Restructuring – review organization structure to remove inefficient layers which contribute to unnecessary costs (Chen, 1985).

3. Marketing – constantly improve marketing methods so that customers are well informed and efficiently served (Whiltington, 1989; Committee for Economic Development, 1954).

4. Improve inventory policy – businesses should adopt a more stable inventory policy. Speculation on inventories should be avoided. A

minimum inventory level needed for efficiency should be maintained (Palmer, 1991; Committee for Economic Development, 1954).

5. Financing – a long-term plan should include provision for financing that is not entirely dependent on current profits (Committee for Economic Development, 1954).

6. Plant and equipment expenditure – leasing rather than purchasing assets offers the potential for maintaining cash-flow flexibility in a business (Morine, 1980).

7. Research and development – companies in decline should not be discouraged from investments in research and development works (Nueno, 1993).

8. Public listing – private companies may want to consider going public to tap a wider capital base (Chen, 1985).

9. Diversification – overseas investments as well as upstream and downstream diversification help to spread risks (Chen, 1985; Whiltington, 1989; Penrose, 1995).

Other Actions

Apart from the above strategic options, firms should also consider other aspects of running their businesses both within and outside their organizations. These include the following:

1. Maintain rapport with developers and suppliers (Low, 1992).
2. Improve employee morale (Low, 1992).
3. Cordial relationships with trade unions (Cordova and Dror, 1984; Townsend, 1983).
4. Regain credibility with customers and suppliers (Slatter, 1992).
5. Retain staff (Cordova and Dror, 1984; Townsend, 1983).

GOING FORWARD

The review above highlighted the strategies that firms may adopt in both good (Low, 1992) (e.g. the 1992 construction boom in Singapore) and bad (Low and Lim, 1999) (e.g. the 1997 Asian financial crisis) times to gain competitive advantage and to plan for long-term survival. Nevertheless, it should be noted that many of the most successful and widely used strategic tools today – the five forces framework, cost curves, the structure-conduct-performance model and the concept of sustainable competitive advantage, to name a few – owed their origins to ideas developed in the 1950s in a field known as the theory of industrial organization. Industrial organization theory, which is concerned with industry structure and firm performance, is in turn based on microeconomics theory.

In the mid-19th century, a group of energy physicists developed a theory of closed equilibrium systems; which provides the core metaphor of Alfred Marshall's traditional economics and much of today's management thinking (Beinhocker, 1997). Consider a ball at the bottom of a bowl. If no energy or mass enters or leaves the bowl – if the system is closed – the ball will sit in equilibrium at its bottom forever. In economics terms, the sides of the bowl represent the structure of a market (for instance, producer costs and consumer preferences), and the gravity that pulls the ball to its lowest energy representing profit seeking behavior at work, and if firms are rational, one can predict where the ball will come to rest in the bowl; in other words, the prices, quantities produced and the profitability of firms under equilibrium. If some external shock hits the system (say a technology shift alters production costs), the sides of the bowl alter its shape and the ball rolls to a new point of equilibrium (Beinhocker, 1997).

In a typical modern strategic analysis, a company looks at its position in the current industry structure, considers the changes that are occurring or might occur in the future, and then develops a point of view on how the industry is likely to change and what that means for its own strategy. Such an approach holds three important assumptions:

1. The industry structure is known.
2. Diminishing returns apply.
3. All firms are perfectly rational.

Considering what would happen if rapid technology or business system innovation makes producers' costs and consumers' preferences uncertain? What if firms lack incomplete information or different firms interpret the same information in multiple different ways?

Should the fundamental assumptions underlying the equilibrium model falters, the effect on the ball in the bowl will be dramatic. The sides of the bowl start to bend and flex, losing their smooth shape and becoming a landscape of troughs and ridges. It is impossible now to predict where the ball will roll and Alfred Marshal loses his equilibrium (Beinhocker, 1997).

Many companies now come to a realization that they can no longer rely on this theory anymore as it holds too much unrealistic constant assumptions, where it does not take into account that environment and market structure are constantly changing. This is because (Beinhocker, 1997):

1. Market and industry structures are open and operate in highly dynamic system, where the energy and mass constantly flow through a complex adaptive system to keep it in its dynamic disequilibrium. On the contrary, the Marshall ball-in-a-bowl system is closed: no energy or mass enters or leaves and the system can settle into an equilibrium state.

2. Systems are made of interacting parties, such as people, dissimilar systems and different business units, creating a relationship of interdependency. Therefore, what each factor does affects one or more of the other agents at least in one way or another. This as a result, creates complexity and makes outcomes difficult to predict.

3. Complex adaptive systems exhibit emergence and self-organization. As individuals alone, people do not do much. But putting them in a group where people can interact, an ant hill emerges.

Taking into account of Alfred Marshall's traditional economics theory, it is now that for almost two decades, managers have been learning to play by a new set of rules that necessitates being nimble and flexible enough to respond rapidly to competition and market changes. They constantly strive to gain effectiveness and nurture a number of core competencies to stay ahead of their rivals. Hence more and more companies are following the path of mutually destructive competition as such strategies are rejected to be too static for today's dynamic markets where new technologies and management approaches are constantly being developed and new inputs become available (Beinhocker, 1997). According to this new dogma, rivals can easily imitate any market position and thus competitive advantage is, at best, temporary unless the company indeed has the capability to compete successfully on the basis of operational effectiveness over an extended period of time - meaning staying ahead of rivals on a daily basis.

The root of the problem is the failure to distinguish between operational effectiveness and strategy. This view is mirrored by Porter (1996, p.61) who stated that "the quest for productivity, quality and speed has spawned a remarkable number of management tools and techniques: total quality management, benchmarking, time-based competition, out-sourcing, partnering and re-engineering." Porter (1996) continued to argue that "it is essential to improve on operational effectiveness but not sufficient enough." As a result,

Porter (1996, p.61) suggested that "rivals could quickly imitate each other, causing strategies to meet into identical paths that no one can win; this frustration is an inability to translate those returns into profitability."

It is now that in the 21st century that economic markets have evolved through periods of relative calm and stability and pushing forward into stormy restructuring periods that makes it all the more complex and thorny for companies to survive for long periods. Similarly, companies have also gone through hard times surviving the upheavals and technological shifts that punctuated the evolution of markets. In other words, the strategy has now deviated away from quality and also operational efficiency. Every company has been there, done that, and got that ISO 9001 certificate. Instead, companies should now be in the era of being different, meaning deliberately choosing a different set of activities to deliver a unique mix of values which sets the company apart from their rivals (Low, 1992).

For these reasons, in this turbulent world today where new business models rapidly supplant old business models, innovation and differentiation must encompass more than just product line extensions and incremental efficiency gains. Today, the unit of analysis for companies should be to examine the entire business systems, i.e. their value chains and activities. Not only that, companies have to constantly be able to ask themselves the fundamental questions of - who are we, how do we compete, which customers do we serve and where are we going to (Porter, 2004)?

In the context of Singapore where the study for this book took place, there has been much criticism directed at the construction industry for being dirty, dangerous and demanding (Construction 21 Steering Committee, 1999) and where many construction firms are still adopting old management business models to survive in the turbulent and modern-day marketplace. This was evident during the 1997 Asian financial crisis that witnessed the collapse of a good number of large contractors. In view of this, there has been an attempt to shift the mindset of the construction industry towards being more progressive, productive and professional instead of dirty, dangerous and demanding.

Consequently, there is an urgent need for continuous improvements. Possibly, radical and innovative changes have to be made to suit the new knowledge-based and knowledge-driven economy so that the construction industry can keep up with sporadic changes in the regional economies. Hence, the main motivation for this book is to examine the behavior that governs the strategic management and performance of large contractors in the construction industry as they compete in the business of contracting.

OBJECTIVES

This book firstly discusses and validates Porter's (1981, 1996, 1998, 2004) three generic strategies for adoption by large construction firms. It then examines if the three generic strategies are mutually exclusive or if these can be adopted jointly. The importance of technology towards creating competitive advantage for the construction firms would also be examined. In the final analysis, possible strategies are proposed for construction firms to improve their current positions relating to competitiveness in the marketplace.

STRUCTURE

A review of Michael Porter's theory of competitive strategy and competitive advantage of firms in a given industry is examined. This is followed by an introduction to the concept of generic strategies – cost leadership, differentiation and focus – to represent the alternative strategic positions in the construction industry, and hence to examine how Porter's (1998, 2004) paradigm would be relevant for construction firms and to make recommendations for suitable competitive strategies.

Based on empirical findings, this book will show how closely the theory relating to generic strategies applies to actual behavior of large construction firms. There are nine chapters in this book, the contents of which are described below.

This chapter provides the background and objectives as well as introduces the theoretical framework for the study in this book. Chapter 2 describes the framework of competitive strategy for analyzing industries and competitors. It also describes three generic strategies for achieving competitive advantage; namely cost leadership, differentiation and focus. Chapter 3 examines the theory of competitive advantage and how a firm can actually deploy the generic strategies in practice based on the literature review presented earlier in Chapter 2. Chapter 4 discusses the possible responses of construction firms based on the marketplace setting in Singapore, in accordance with the theoretical espousal described in Chapter 3. Chapter 5 briefly highlights the research methodology adopted to garner empirical evidence for the study in Singapore. The profile and characteristics of the construction firms, the interviewees and their respective projects in the Singapore construction industry would be highlighted. Chapter 6 presents the empirical findings with the corresponding results and discussions. The analysis examines the responses of construction firms, including their long term objectives and strategies and how the various strategies had benefitted them or placed them in a disadvantaged situation. This chapter focuses on differentiation, focus and cost advantage as observed to being practiced by construction firms in Singapore. Chapter 7 is a continuation of Chapter 6 but with an emphasis on the hybrid strategies as observed to being practiced by construction firms in Singapore. Chapter 8 is an extension of Chapters 6 and 7 which describes a case study of a large construction firm in Singapore. Its purpose is to examine the relevance of the competitive theories proposed by Porter (1998, 2004) in the construction industry. Chapter 9 concludes the study with a proposal for enhancing the performance of the industry structure as well as a review of the strategic management of construction firms. The limitations of the study and recommendations for future studies are presented in this chapter.

Chapter 2

COMPETITIVE STRATEGY

A NEW PARADIGM

There has been a growing acceptance that the assumptions underlying the theories of comparative advantage appear to be unrealistic in many industries. This is because the so-called standard paradigm assumes that there are no economies of scale, that technology everywhere are identical and that products are undifferentiated. In actual fact, all these assumptions bear little relation to the realities seen in most industries.

CHANGING COMPETITION

In the eighteenth and nineteenth centuries, when many industries were fragmented, when production focused on cheap labor and less skill-intensive processes, the reliance was then on natural resources and capital. Furthermore, factor costs remain to be an important consideration in industries that are dependent on natural resources, wherein unskilled or semi-skilled labor is the dominant contributor to total costs and where technology is simple and widely available. This happened when the world experienced the Industrial Revolution, when more and more industries began to ameliorate their operations to become more knowledge intensive and the role of factor costs has turned out to be an obstacle in the face of a rapidly changing environment (Serpell and Ocaranza, 2001).

TECHNOLOGICAL CHANGE

Economies were widespread; most products are differentiated where technological change is pervasive and continuous. Technology has provided the key to overcome scarce factors via new products and processes. It has nullified or reduced the importance of certain factors of production that once loomed large, whereby technology and skills today have supplant the importance of these factors by processing them more effectively and efficiently (Serpell and Ocaranza, 2001).

GLOBALIZATION

Competition in many industries has internationalized, where firms compete with truly global strategies involving selling worldwide and sourcing components and materials worldwide. The outcome of globalization has therefore led to raw materials, components, machinery and many services to be available globally on comparable terms (Serpell and Ocaranza, 2001).

COMPETITION

The essence for understanding competition is the industry. In this context, an industry (whether relating to products or services) is a group of competitors producing products or services that compete directly with each other. These concepts apply equally to both products and services (Porter, 1998, 2004).

The intensity of competition in any industry is neither caused by a stroke of luck nor a mere coincidence; instead it is entrenched in its underlying economic structure and goes beyond the behavior of current competitors. Hence, competitive strategy involves a sophisticated understanding of the structure of the industry and how it is changing. Porter (1998, 2004) suggests that in any given industry, domestic or international, the nature and strength of competition is embodied in five competitive forces. These forces which drive industry competition include: (a) the threat of new entrants (b) the threat of substitute products or services (c) the bargaining power of suppliers (d) the bargaining power of buyers, and (e) the rivalry among the existing competitors.

The joint strength of these forces determines the ultimate profit potential in the industry, where profit potential is measured in terms of long run return on invested capital. Thus the goal of a competitive strategy for any business unit in an industry is to seek a position in the industry where the company can best defend itself against these competitive forces or can influence them in its favor. Comprehending these sources allows firms to identify their critical strengths and weaknesses of the business, consider their positioning in their industry, locate the areas where strategic changes may yield the greatest payoff and direct attention to the areas where industry trends promise to hold the greatest significance as either opportunities or threats (Porter, 1998, 2004).

Threat of Entry

New entrants to an industry bring new capacity, the motivation to gain market share and usually considerable resources. The threat of entry into an industry depends on the strength of barriers to entry that are present, coupled with the reaction from existing competitors that the entrant can expect. For instance, if the barriers are high, then the new entrant can expect strong retaliation from established rivals; the threat of entry is perceived to be low (Porter, 1998, 2004).

Intensity of Rivalry among Existing Competitors

. , Rivalry among existing competitors takes the familiar form of haggling for position – by means of similar tactics like price competition, advertising battle, new product introduction and increased customer service or warranties. This usually occurs because one or more competitors are either pressurized to do so or views the prospect to improve its position. In most industries, competitive moves by one firm have considerable impacts on its competitors and thus may provoke retaliation or effort to counter the move; that is, firms are mutually dependent.

Porter (1998, 2004) attributed this to a number of interacting factors leading to intense rivalry such as numerous or equally balanced competitors, slow industry growth, high fixed or storage costs, lack of differentiation or switching costs, capacity augmented in large increments, diverse competitors, high strategic stakes and high exit barriers. These factors will be discussed further.

Pressure from Substitute Products

All firms in an industry are competing, in a broad sense, with industries producing substitute products. Substitutes limit the potential returns of an industry by placing a ceiling on the prices that firms in the industry can profitably charge. Profits will be further stretched as a result of increasingly competitive prices.

Identifying substitute products is to search for other products that can perform the same function as the product of the industry. Securities brokers, for example, are being threatened by substitutes such as real estate, insurance, money market funds and other ways for the individual to invest capital, accentuated in importance by the poor performance of the equity markets (Porter, 1998, 2004).

Bargaining Power of Buyers

Buyers compete with the industry by driving down prices, demanding for higher quality or more services and playing competitors against each other in cut-throat situations – all at the risk of industry profitability. The power of each of the industry's important buyer groups depends on a number of characteristics of its market situation and on the relative importance of its purchases from the industry compared with its overall business (Porter, 1998, 2004).

Bargaining Power of Suppliers

Suppliers can wield bargaining power over participants in an industry by threatening to increase prices or reduce the quality of goods and services. Powerful suppliers – particularly when the market place is dominated by a few large companies and/or the suppliers' goods and services is a significant input to the buyer's business, thus allow suppliers to thereby squeeze profitability out of an industry; individual firms are unable to recover costs despite increasing its own price (Porter, 1998, 2004).

STRUCTURAL ANALYSIS AND COMPETITIVE STRATEGY

Once the forces affecting competition in an industry and their underlying causes have been analyzed, the firm is in a position to recognize its own strengths and weaknesses relative to the industry. An effective competitive strategy incorporates either offensive or defensive action in order to create an invulnerable position against the five competitive forces. Porter (1998, 2004) had examined a number of the possible approaches as described below.

Positioning

Knowing the company's own capabilities and resources as well as the causes of the competitive forces will highlight the areas where and when the company should confront competition and where and when to avoid it (Porter, 1998, 2004).

Influencing the Balance

A company can develop a strategy that takes the offensive that is intended to do more than merely cope with the forces themselves such as through innovations and capital investments. Structural analysis can also be used to make out what are the key forces influencing competition and in turn places the firm in a strategic position where the forces are the weakest in order to yield the maximum payoff (Porter, 1998, 2004).

Exploiting Change

Industry evolution is important strategically because evolution naturally alters in the face of competition. What was viable in the past has the potential to fail today as the industry becomes more mature and may also drive smaller and inefficient firms out of business. These business trends alone are not so vital; the key is to find out whether these trends had affected the forces of competition. Such analysis can also be used to predict and establish the profitability of the industry. In the long run, the consideration is to examine each underlying competitive force, predict the degree of each cause and then to create a composite representation of the possible profit potential of the industry (Porter, 1998, 2004).

Diversification Strategy

The framework for analyzing industry competition can be used in diversification strategy, which allows the firm to spot a potential of its business in the industry by helping to identity valuable types of relatedness in diversification (Porter, 1998, 2004).

GENERIC COMPETITIVE STRATEGIES

Firms discovered many different approaches and the best strategy for a given firm is ultimately a unique construction of strategic positioning. However, at the broadest level, Porter (1998, 2004) had identified three consistent generic strategies for creating such an invulnerable position and outperforming competitors in an industry in the long run.

Overall Cost Leadership

The first strategy popularized in the 1970s is set by achieving overall cost leadership in the industry. Cost leadership requires aggressive structure of efficient facilities, vigorous pursuit of cost reductions from experience, tight cost and strict overheads control, avoidance of marginal customer accounts and cost minimization in areas like research and development, service, sales force and so on. Low cost relative to competitors becomes the central premise running through the entire corporate strategy from quality to service (Porter, 1998, 2004).

Attaining a low-cost position does not mean that the firm is yielding a meagre profit margin. On the contrary, the firm is able to achieve an above-average return on investments because its lower costs means that the firm can still earn returns even after all its rivals have competed away their profits through rivalry (Porter, 1998, 2004).

Differentiation

Differentiation is brought about by creating the uniqueness of the product or service offered by the firm. If achieved, differentiation is a viable strategy for securing above-average returns in an industry because it creates a defensible position for coping with the five competitive forces, albeit in a different way than cost leadership (Porter, 1998, 2004). Moreover, differentiation softens competitive rivalry because of brand loyalty by customers who are less sensitive to price.

Focus

The final generic strategy rests on a particular buyer group or segment of the product line which the entire focus strategy is built around serving a particular target very well. The strategy rests on the premise that the firm has the ability to serve its narrow strategic target more effectively and efficiently than competitors who are competing more broadly. Thus the adoption of the focus strategy appears to be appropriate only for the smaller firms. Subsequently, the firm achieves either differentiation from better meeting the needs of the particular target or lower costs in serving this target (Porter, 1998, 2004).

In grand summary, the strategic advantage may be attributed at the industry-wide level or at a particular segment of the industry only. At the industry-wide level, the strategic advantage may be attained through uniqueness perceived by the customer (i.e. differentiation) or through a low cost position (i.e. overall cost leadership). For a particular segment of the industry, for example, the public housing sector in the construction industry, strategic advantage may be attained through focus.

STRATEGIES FOR BUYERS AND SUPPLIERS

Policies directed at both the buyers and suppliers are often neglected or looked at too narrowly, with the primary focus on operating problems. Yet in the adaptation of the broader perspective of strategy towards buyers and suppliers, the firm may be able to improve its competitive position and reduce its vulnerability to the industry structure (Porter, 1998, 2004).

Buyer Selection

Most industries sell their products or services not to just a single buyer but to a variety of buyers. One of the key competitive forces determining the potential profitability of an industry is the bargaining power of this group of buyers. In this context, the firm should therefore sell to the most favorable buyers possible, to the extent it has any choice. Buyer selection plays a vital role in the growth rate of the firm and can mitigate any disruptive power of buyers. Buyer selection with emphasis to structural considerations is an especially pertinent strategic variable in mature industries and in those where the barriers caused by product differentiation or technological innovations are hard to sustain (Porter, 1998, 2004).

Framework for Buyer Selection and Strategy

There are four broad criteria that determine the quality of buyers from a strategic standpoint (Porter, 1998, 2004):

1. Purchasing needs versus company capabilities
2. Growth potential
3. Structural position
   a. Intrinsic bargaining power
   b. Propensity to exercise this bargaining power in demanding low prices
4. Cost of servicing

The firm will improve its competitive advantage, other things being equal, if it targets towards buyers whose particular needs the firm is in the best relative position to serve.

Purchasing Strategy

The analysis of the power of the suppliers as mentioned earlier coupled with a reverse application of the principles of buyer selection can help a firm to formulate an appropriate purchasing strategy. Key issues pertaining to the formulation of purchasing strategy have been identified (Porter, 1998, 2004) which relate to:

1. Stability and competitiveness of the supplier pool
2. Optimal degree of vertical integration
3. Allocation of purchases among qualified suppliers
4. Creation of maximum leverage with chosen suppliers

In purchasing, the central goal then is to find the means to lower and improve the bargaining position of the firm by overcoming the suppliers' power in order to reduce the total costs of purchasing. In some cases, this power is built into industry economics and is out of the firm's control. In many cases, however, it can be mitigated through strategy.

STRUCTURAL ANALYSIS WITHIN THE INDUSTRY

The five broad competitive forces provide the context in which all firms in an industry compete. However, there remains a need to explain why some firms are persistently more profitable than others and how this relates to their strategic choice. There is a need to understand how firms have different competencies in marketing, cost cutting, management, organization, and so on. There is also a need to relate how their current strategic postures, coupled with the existing industry structure, would in turn be translated into performance in the marketplace. The concepts presented below will explain the differences in the performance of firms in the same industry and at the same time, provides a framework for guiding the choice of a competitive strategy (Porter, 1998, 2004).

Dimensions of Competitive Strategy

The strategies of companies for competing in an industry can differ broadly. The following are some of the possible differences among company strategic options in a given industry (Porter, 1998, 2004):

1. Specialization
2. Brand identification
3. Push versus pull production system
4. Channel selection
5. Product quality
6. Technological leadership
7. Cost position
8. Price policy
9. Relationship with parent company

Each of these strategic dimensions can be described for a firm at differing levels and other dimensions might be added to refine the analysis; the pertinent thing is that these dimensions help to provide an overall picture of the firm's strategic position.

Strategic Groups

The first step in structural analysis is to characterize the strategies of all significant competitors. A strategic group belongs to a group of firms in an industry applying the same or similar strategy. An industry could hypothetically have only one strategic group if all the firms technically followed the same strategy; at the extreme end, each firm could be in a different strategic group. Often, there are a small number of strategic groups which captures the essence of strategic differences in the industry (Porter, 1998, 2004). In this context, a hypothetical industry may reflect specialization along a spectrum that denotes full line specialization and narrow line specialization. Various strategic groups may be mapped within the hypothetical industry to include, for example:

1. Group A: with full line, low manufacturing costs, low service and moderate quality.
2. Group B: with narrow line, high price, high technology and high quality.
3. Group C: with moderate line, medium price, very high customer service, low quality and low price.
4. Group D: with narrow line, high automation and low price (Porter, 1998, 2004).

The classification of various firms into strategic groups is designed to aid in structural analysis. Arguably, every firm is unique and the actual profitability of each individual firm would also differ from each other in the long run due to their ability to implement and execute those common strategies.

Mobility Barriers

The same underlying economic principles contributing to barriers to entry can also be framed more generally as mobility barriers that prevent the firms from moving from one strategic position to another. Hence this is why mobility barriers provide the first major reason why some firms in an industry are persistently more profitable than others. Without mobility barriers, even firms with successful strategies will be quickly imitated by others and the firm's profitability will tend towards equality except for differences in their abilities to execute the best strategy in an operational sense. The existence of mobility barriers means that some firms are able to enjoy some advantages over the rest, through economies of scales, cost advantages and so on, which are extremely difficult to overcome.

As with entry barriers, mobility barriers can also change. As they change, some firms may choose to abandon some strategic groups and venture into new ones. In addition, mobility barriers can also be influenced by the choice of strategy adopted by firms, through advertising, for instance, to develop brand identification to create a new strategic group (Porter, 1998, 2004).

Bargaining Power

Just as different strategies are protected by differing mobility barriers, firms enjoy differing degrees of bargaining power with suppliers or customers for two reasons. Firstly, their strategies may yield them differing degrees of vulnerability to common suppliers or buyers; and secondly their strategies may involve dealing with different suppliers or buyers with corresponding different levels of bargaining power (Porter, 1998, 2004).

Rivalry among Firms

The presence of more than one strategic group in an industry will generally intensify rivalry because it implies greater diversity or asymmetry among firms in the industry that will have the tendency to complicate their understanding of each others' intentions and reacting to them. According to Porter (1998, 2004), this will thus increase the likelihood of repeated outbreaks of conflicts.

Not all differences in strategy will significantly affect industrial rivalry. Some firms are affected more by hard-nosed price cutting whereas others are affected by other forms of rivalry. Four factors can be used to determine the strength the strategic groups in any specific industry will interact with in competing for customers:

1. Market interdependence among groups
2. Product differentiation achieved by the groups
3. Number of strategic groups and their relative sizes
4. Strategic distance among groups (Porter, 1998, 2004)

Strategic groups can also be affected by the patterns of rivalry within the industry, which is similar to the concept of strategic group mapping based on specialization for a hypothetical industry described earlier. The exception is that the horizontal axis is now the target customer segments of the strategic group measuring market interdependence. In this context, the vertical axis represents key strategic dimensions in the industry which mirrors inter-group rivalry. Strategic groups, with their size proportional to the market share, may be mapped using different sizes of circles, triangles and boxes, etc. The shape of the groups is used to represent their overall strategic configuration, with differences in shape representing strategic distance. In strategic group mapping, Groups A, D, F and G may for example be enclosed by circles of different size. Likewise, Groups C and E may be enclosed by triangles of different size. Group B may be enclosed by a box. Applying the analysis presented earlier, Group D, for example, can be much less affected by industry rivalry than Group A; being further away from each other. Group A competes with similarly large Groups B and C, who use different strategies to reach the same basic customer segment. Firms in this strategic group will be constantly engaged in conflicts. Groups E and F, who are smaller, could be viewed as "specialist" firms (Porter, 1998, 2004).

Chapter 3

COMPETITIVE ADVANTAGE

INTRODUCTION

Competitive advantage is at the heart of a firm's performance in competitive markets. Firms throughout the world face slower growth; domestic and global competitors are not spared in that they no longer act as if the expanding pie were big enough for all. Hence, this almost creates a mandatory need for firms to create and sustain a competitive advantage. This is because, quite often, the strategies of many firms failed due to their inability to translate a broad competitive strategy into specific action steps required in gaining competitive advantage. In this context, this chapter shall examine how understanding the concept of competitive advantage can help firms put in place their generic strategies (Porter, 1998, 2004).

Instead of just examining one aspect of the firm, this chapter will cut across the many disciplines to provide a more holistic view of the entire supply chain of the firm. These would range from marketing, production, control and finance to many other activities in a firm where each plays a role in contributing to competitive advantage.

COMPETITIVE ADVANTAGE PRINCIPLES

The competitive advantage of a firm grows fundamentally on the firm's ability to create value for its buyers. It may take the form of prices that are lower than the competitors for equivalent benefits or the provision of unique benefits that comes with a premium price. In this chapter, the term value chain will be a recurring theme, to distinguish between buyers, suppliers and a firm in discrete but interrelated activities from which value stems and which would, in turn, relate to how these activities are linked to the buyer's value.

Value Chain and Competitive Advantage

The value chain of each individual firm derives from multiple discrete activities from designing, producing, marketing, and delivering to supporting its product. Each of these activities can add on to a firm's relative cost position and create a basis for potential sources of differentiation. A firm can realize competitive advantage by performing these strategically important activities at a lower cost or better than its competitors (Porter, 1998, 2004).

A firm's value chain may differ from that of its competitors, representing an opportunity for a source of competitive advantage. It is therefore essential to understand the role of the value chain in order to identify the sources of competitive advantage.

The Value Chain

The value chain consists of nine generic categories of activities that are meant to design, deliver, market, deliver, and support its product. Although most firms in the same industry can expect to share similar chains, the value chains of competitors often differ. For this reason, differences among competitors' value chains are a valuable source of competitive advantage.

In competitive terms, the value is the amount buyers are willing to pay for the product or service. It is measured by total revenue, a reflection of the price a firm's product commands and the units it can sell. A profitable firm happens when the value it commands exceeds the costs involved in creating the product. Hence, the objective of a firm is to create value for buyers that exceed the cost of doing so. Value, instead of cost, must be used in analyzing competitive position since firms often deliberately raise their costs in order to command a premium price via differentiation (Porter, 1998, 2004).

The generic value chain displays total value which consists of value activities and margins. Value activities are the physically and technologically distinct activities a firm performs. These are the building blocks by which a firm creates a product valuable to its buyers. Every value chain needs to employ purchased inputs, human resources (labor and management), and some forms of technology to perform its function. Each value activity also utilizes and creates information, such as buyer data (order entry), performance parameters (testing), and product failure statistics. Value activities may also create financial assets such as inventory and accounts receivable, or liabilities such as accounts payable.

Value activities can be divided into two broad categories in the generic value chain: primary activities and support activities. Primary activities are the activities involved in the physical creation of the product and its sale and transfer to the buyer as well as after-sales assistance. In any firm, primary activities can be divided into the five generic categories that include inbound logistics, operations, outbound logistics, marketing and sales, as well as service. Support activities provide support to the primary activities through the provision of purchased inputs, technology, human resources and various firm-wide functions. Certain aspects of procurement, technology development and human resource management can be associated with specific primary activities as well as support the entire chain. The infrastructure of the firm is not associated with any particular primary activities but supports the entire value chain. The value chain of any firm is therefore the fundamental building blocks of competitive advantage. The performance of primary activities and support activities would determine the firm's margin. How each activity is performed combined with its economics will determine whether a firm is high or low cost relative to its competitors. How each value activity is performed will also determine its contribution to the buyer's needs and hence differentiation. Comparing the value chains of competitors would expose differences that determine competitive advantage (Porter, 1998, 2004). Economists have characterized the firm as having a production function that defines how inputs are converted into outputs. The value chain theory views the firm as a collection of discrete but related production functions, if production functions are defined as activities. The value chain formulation focuses on how these activities create value and what determines their costs, giving the firm considerable latitude in determining how activities are configured and combined (Porter, 1998, 2004).

An analysis of the value chain rather than value added therefore appears to be a more appropriate way to examine competitive advantage; this is because the latter tends to associate raw materials from the many other purchased inputs used in a firm's activities. In addition, the cost behavior of activities cannot be understood without simultaneously examining the costs of the inputs used to perform them. Moreover, value added fails to highlight the linkages between a firm and its suppliers that can reduce costs or enhance differentiation (Porter, 1998, 2004).

Defining the Value Chain

To diagnose competitive advantage, it is necessary to define a firm's value in a particular industry. Beginning with a generic chain, individual value activities are identified in the particular firm. To reiterate, it was noted that the primary activities in the generic value chain would include the inbound logistics, operations, outbound logistics, marketing and sales, as well as service. In sub-dividing a generic value chain, for example, marketing and sales may in turn focus on marketing management, advertising, sales force administration, production of technical literature and sales promotion. This sub-division would apply to all the primary activities and support activities of the generic value chain to yield the following.

In the case of primary activities, sub-division may take place as follows:

1. Inbound logistics – dealing with inbound material handling, inbound inspection, parts picking and delivery, etc.
2. Operations – dealing with fabrication of components, assembly, fine tuning and testing, maintenance, etc.
3. Outbound logistics – dealing with order processing, shipping, etc.
4. Marketing and sales – dealing with advertising, sales promotion, sales force administration, etc.
5. Service – dealing with service representatives, systems for spare parts management, etc.

In the case of support activities, sub-division may take place as follows, with the primary activities which the sub-divisions serve indicated in brackets:

1. Human resource management – dealing with recruitment (for Operations, Marketing and sales, and Service) and training (for Operations).
2. Technology development – dealing with the design of automated systems (for Inbound logistics); component design, design of assembly lines, machine design, testing procedures and energy management (for Operations); information system development and computer service (for Outbound logistics); market research, sales aides and media agency services (for Marketing and sales); and service manuals and procedures as well as management of spare parts (for Service).
3. Procurement – dealing with transportation services (for both Inbound and Outbound logistics); materials, energy, other parts and supplies (for Operations); travel and subsistence as well as supplies (for Marketing and sales); and travel and subsistence (for Service).

The above illustration demonstrates an example of a complete value chain of a typical firm, where the value activities are assigned to categories that best represent their contributions to a firm's competitive advantage (Porter, 1998, 2004).

Linkages within the Value Chain

The value chain is not a collection of independent activities. Rather it is a system of interdependent activities; they are related by linkages within the value chain. Linkages are relationships between the way one value activity is performed and the cost or performance of another. Thus, competitive advantage frequently derives from linkages among activities as it does from the individual activities themselves in two ways (Porter, 1998, 2004).

Firstly, linkages often reflect tradeoffs among activities to achieve the same overall result. For instance, more costly material specifications may reduce service costs. Therefore, a firm must optimize such linkages to reflect its strategies in order to achieve competitive advantages.

Secondly, the linkages may also reflect the need to coordinate activities. On-time delivery often requires stringent coordination of activities in operations, outbound logistics and service. The ability to coordinate linkages often reduces costs or enhances differentiation. As a result, linkages imply that a firm's cost of differentiation is not merely the result of efforts to reduce costs or improve performance in each value activity individually. Much of the change shows the positive attitude towards quality which is indirectly recognizing the importance of linkages.

Although it is undeniable that linkages within the value chain are crucial to competitive advantage, they are often subtle and may often go unrecognized.

The Buyer's Value Chain

According to Porter (1998, 2004), buyers too have their own value chain and a firm's product represents a purchased input to the buyer's value chain. A firm's differentiation stems from how its value chain relates to its buyer's value chain. This is a function of the way a firm's physical product is used in the particular buyer's activity in which it is consumed as well as all the other points of contact between a firm's value chain and the buyer's value chain. For example, this may include how the firm works closely with the buyer in designing a particular product. Such contact point is essentially a potential source of differentiation. Therefore, it would appear from here that the word "quality" is too narrow a view of what makes a firm unique, because it focuses attention on the product rather than the broader array of value activities that impact the buyer (Porter, 1998, 2004).

Differentiation then fundamentally derives from creating value for the buyer and must be perceived to be valuable by the buyer if it is to be rewarded with a premium price.

VALUE CHAIN AND ORGANIZATIONAL STRUCTURE

The value chain is a basic instrument for diagnosing, creating and sustaining competitive advantage. Furthermore, the chain also plays a valuable role in designing organizational structure which creates individual divisions within a firm by grouping certain activities together such as finance or production so that similar activities should be exploited by grouping them in a department. By the same token, at the same time, dissimilar activities should be separated from other groups of activities.

Frequently, there are multiple linkages within the value chain and yet organizational structure often fails to provide the mechanisms to coordinate or optimize them. Moreover, the managers of support activities do not have a clear view of how these linkages relate to the firm's overall competitive position, something that the value chain highlights. An organizational structure that corresponds to the value chain will therefore improve a firm's ability to create and sustain competitive advantage (Porter, 1998, 2004).

COST ADVANTAGE

Many companies recognize the importance of costs and have many strategic plans in place that revolve around "cost leadership" or "cost reduction". Typical cost studies tend to concentrate on production costs and overlook the impact of other activities such as marketing, after-sales service, and infrastructure on the relative cost position. The pertinent factor for firms to take note is the identification of cost drivers. These are the structural determinants of the cost of an activity and differ in the extent to which a firm controls them (Porter, 1998, 2004). Cost drivers determine the behavior of costs within an activity, reflecting any linkages or interrelationships that affect it. A firm's cost performance in each of its major discrete activities cumulates to establish its relative cost position.

Value Chain and Cost Analysis

A cost analysis seeks to examine costs within these activities and not the costs of the firm as a whole. Each value activity has its own cost structure and how the behavior of its cost may be affected by linkages and interrelationships with other activities both within and outside the firm. Cost advantage results if the firm achieves a lower cumulative cost of performing value activities than its competitors (Porter, 1998, 2004).

Defining Value Chain for Cost Analysis

The starting point for cost analysis is to define a firm's value chain and assigning operating costs and assets to its value activities. Each activity in the value chain involves both operating costs and assets in the firm in terms of fixed and working capital. For instance, purchased inputs make up part of the costs of every value activity and can contribute to both operating costs and assets.

For the purposes of cost analysis, there are three generic principles that reflect their impact these have on the value chain. It is cautioned that these are not mutually exclusive:

1. The size and growth of the cost represented by the activity.
2. The cost behavior of the activity.
3. Competitor is different in performing the activity.

Activities should be separated for cost analysis if they represent a significant or rapidly growing percentage of operating costs or assets. Most firms often overlooked the minor but growing value activities that can eventually change their cost structure (Porter, 1998, 2004).

COST BEHAVIOR

A firm's cost position results from the cost behavior of its value activities. Cost behavior depends on a number of factors that influence cost – cost drivers. The important cost driver or drivers can differ among firms even in the same industry if they employ different value chains. A firm's relative cost position in a value activity depends on its standing vis-à-vis important cost drivers (Porter, 1998, 2004).

Cost Drivers

Porter (1998, 2004) identified ten major cost drivers that determine the cost behavior of value activities: economies of scale, learning and the pattern of capacity utilization, linkages, integration, interrelationships, timing, discretionary policies, location and institutional factors. Cost drivers are the structural causes of the cost of an activity and can be more or less under a firm's control. More importantly, the relative impact of cost drivers will differ among value activities along the value chain. Thus no one cost driver is ever the sole determinant of a firm's cost position. For this reason, diagnosing the cost drivers of each value activity allows a firm to gain a greater understanding of the sources of its relative cost position and how it might be changed (Porter, 1998, 2004).

Diagnosing Cost Drivers

The cost behavior of a value activity can be a function of more than one cost driver. While one driver may exert the strongest influence on the cost of a value activity, several cost drivers often interact to determine costs. Thus, it is imperative for firms to establish the relationships between cost drivers and the cost of a value activity whenever possible, in order to determine the relative significance of each cost driver. In addition, identifying interactions among cost drivers are necessary for determining the cost behavior of a value activity. Where drivers are reinforcing, a firm must coordinate its strategy to achieve the lowest possible cost. Interactions among cost drivers are often subtle in that these have frequently gone unrecognized. Hence, the ability to translate insight about the interaction of cost drivers into strategic choices can thus be an invariable source of cost advantage (Porter, 1998, 2004).

Costs of Purchased Inputs

Procurement has strategic significance in almost every industry. Every value activity employs purchased inputs of some kind, ranging from raw materials, to office space and capital goods. The total costs of purchased inputs as a percentage of a firm's value provide an important indicator of the strategic importance of procurement. In many industries, the total costs of purchased inputs can be an enormous percentage value, yet these receive much less attention than reducing labor costs. In some instances, a firm may lower total costs by spending more on purchased inputs. Minimizing the unit cost of purchased inputs does not always guarantee a cost advantage position for the firm (Porter, 1998, 2004).

An analysis of the purchases made by firms, in general, would focus on the most viable items, especially raw materials and components. Nonetheless, other purchased inputs over and above such raw materials and components, can often constitute an even greater percentage of the costs expended.

Purchasing Information

Porter (1998, 2004) explained that a firm should begin by identifying all major purchased inputs and determining its expenditure on these items on a regular basis. All identified purchased inputs should be listed in the order of importance to total costs so that attention can be focused to areas where opportunities for cost reduction are frequently present. This is because managers have the tendency to focus their attention on those few purchases that represent a significant percentage of costs. As a result, suppliers commonly capitalize on purchases that represent small costs to generate their highest margins.

In this context, the purchasing department will then be responsible for the procedures, procurement expertise and systems for tracking the costs of purchases.

DRIVERS OF PURCHASED INPUT COSTS

In terms of cost dynamics, a firm must consider how the absolute and relative costs of value activities will change over time independent of its strategy (Porter, 1998, 2004). This will enable the firm to forecast how the cost drivers of value activities may change and which value activities will fluctuate in absolute or relative costs importance. A firm with insight into cost dynamics may be able to put themselves in a favorable position to gain cost advantage by anticipating these changes and moving swiftly to respond to them.

Cost Advantage

A firm is said to have achieved a cost advantage position when its cumulative cost of performing all value activities is lower than the competitors' costs. The strategic value of cost advantage hinges on its sustainability over the long term; it will be present if sources of a firm's cost advantage are difficult for competitors to replicate or imitate.

A firm's relative cost position is a function of:

1. The composition of its value chain versus those of the competitors'.
2. Its relative position vis-à-vis the cost drivers of each activity.

Competitors have value chains that may be similar or different from the firm's. If the competitors' value chains are different from that of the firm's, the inherent efficiency of the two value chains will determine the relative cost position. By the same token, a firm's relative cost position in value activities that are the same as those of the competitors' would depend on the firm's position vis-à-vis the cost drivers of those activities relative to the competitors (Porter, 1998, 2004). Therefore, a firm should assess the relative cost positions of common value activities, one by one, and then accumulate these together with the relative costs of different activities to determine the overall cost position.

Determining Relative Costs of Competitors

The value chain is an indispensable tool for determining competitors' costs. The first step in determining competitors' costs is to identify the competitor value chains and how activities are performed by them. In practice, it may not be easy to assess competitors' costs because the firm does not have direct access to such information. Consequently, it is usually possible to estimate directly the costs of some competitor's value activities from commonly available public data as well as from relationships with buyers, suppliers and others. Although the competitor's costs cannot be estimated directly, this can remain extremely useful since the firm can combine the available information of each value activity to construct a general picture of a competitor's relative cost position (Porter, 1998, 2004).

Gaining Cost Advantage

Porter (1998, 2004) suggested two major ways in which a firm can gain cost advantage:

1.   Control cost drivers. A firm can gain an advantage with respect to the linkages of cost drivers in the value activities.
2.   Reconfigure the value chain. A firm can adopt a radical and more efficient way to design, produce, distribute or market the product.

These two sources are not mutually exclusive. Successful cost leaders usually derive their cost advantage from multiple sources within the value chain. Sustainable cost advantage stems not from just one activity and reconfiguring the chain frequently plays a role in creating cost advantage. Cost leadership requires meticulous and consistent inspection of every activity in a firm for opportunities to reduce cost. Moreover, every firm should aggressively pursue cost reduction in activities that do not influence differentiation (Porter, 1998, 2004). On the other hand, in activities that contribute to differentiation, a conscious choice may still be made to sacrifice all or part of differentiation in favor of improving the relative cost position.

Sustainability of Cost Advantage

Cost advantage will result in above-average performance only if the firm can sustain it, particularly in the face of entry or mobility barriers that prevent competitors from imitating its sources. Sustainability can vary for different cost drivers and from one industry to another (Porter, 1998, 2004).

Implementation and Cost Advantage

An understanding of how firms can achieve a cost advantage through changes in strategy and the way activities are performed is crucial. Nevertheless, the success of cost leadership is still very much dependent on the skills of a firm in actual implementation and execution on a day to day basis. Firms differ in their abilities to lower costs, despite having similar policies. Improving the relative cost position may not require a major shift in strategy so much as greater management attention. Most importantly, Porter (1998, 2004) cautioned that a firm should never rest on its laurels and assume its costs are low enough. This is because no cost driver works automatically but rather come about as a result of hard work and undivided attention.

DIFFERENHTIATION

Several authors (Porter, 2004; Helms, Clay and Peter, 1997; Jackson, 1989) agreed that a firm differentiates itself from its competitors if it can be unique at something that is valuable to buyers beyond simply offering a low price. Despite the importance of differentiation, it would appear that firms view the potential sources of differentiation too narrowly. They see differentiation in terms of the physical products or marketing practices that set themselves apart from their competitors, rather than differentiation that may potentially arise anywhere along the value chain. Likewise, firms are also often different but not differentiated because they pursue forms of uniqueness that are not appreciated by the buyer (Porter, 1998, 2004).

Sources of Differentiation

Differentiation allows the firm to command a premium price, to sell more of its product at a given price or gain equivalent benefits such as greater buyer loyalty even during economic downturns (Porter, 2004; Chan and Mauborgne, 1999; Wright, 1996).

Differentiation and the Value Chain

Virtually any value activity is a potential source of uniqueness (Porter, 1998, 2004). Take for instance the procurement of raw materials through the primary and support activities and downstream activities. The benefits reaped from differentiation would require consistency or coordination among activities if a firm is to achieve these benefits.

Drivers of Uniqueness

As noted earlier, a firm's uniqueness in a value activity is determined by a series of basic drivers. Exclusivity drivers are the underlying reasons why an activity is unique. Without identifying these exclusivity drivers, a firm cannot fully develop means of creating new forms of differentiation or detect how sustainable its existing differentiation is. The principal uniqueness drivers would include the following: policy choices, linkages, learning spillovers, integration and scale (Porter, 1998, 2004).

The drivers of uniqueness vary for each activity and across industries for the same activity. The interaction of drivers can determine the extent to which an activity is unique. A firm must therefore examine what lies beneath the driver or drivers in each of its areas of uniqueness. This would be critical towards supporting the sustainability of differentiation because some uniqueness drivers provide more sustainability than others (Porter, 1998, 2004).

Costs of Differentiation

Differentiation is usually costly so much so that a firm must often incur costs to be unique because uniqueness requires that it performs value activities better than competitors, such as providing superior engineering applications or greater product durability. The costs of differentiation reflect the cost drivers of the value activities on which the uniqueness is based. The relationship between uniqueness and cost drivers can take two related forms (Porter, 1998, 2004):

1. What makes an activity unique can impact cost drivers.
2. The cost drivers can affect the costs of being unique.

In pursuit of differentiation, a firm often affects the cost drivers of an activity adversely and deliberately adds to costs. At the same time, because uniqueness often increases costs by affecting the cost drivers, the cost drivers then determine how costly differentiation would be. A firm's position vis-à-vis cost drivers would determine how costly a particular differentiation strategy will be relative to the competitors. Hence, the cost drivers play an important role in determining the success of differentiation strategies and have important competitive implications.

As noted earlier, differentiation can be costly. But making an activity unique may also simultaneously lower cost, where integration may render the activity unique and also lower costs if integration is a cost driver. Such a situation, if it arises, may suggest that (a) the firm has been fully exploiting all the opportunities to lower costs; (b) being unique in an activity was formerly deemed to be undesirable; or (c) a breakthrough in innovation that no competitors have adopted, such as a new automated process that both lowers cost and improves quality (Porter, 1998, 2004). Hence the possibility of simultaneously raising differentiation and reducing costs through linkages exist. However, this situation may possibly arise because the firm has not been fully exploiting cost reduction opportunities and not because differentiation is not costly (Porter, 1998, 2004).

Buyer Value and Differentiation

Uniqueness does not automatically equate to differentiation unless it is of value to the buyer. A successful differentiator finds ways and means to generate value for buyers that yield a price premium in excess of the additional costs. In order to understand what is valuable to the buyer, it is important to recognize that the starting point lies with the buyer's value chain. The buyer's value chain determines the manner in which a firm's product is actually used as well as the other effects on the buyer's activities. The firm needs to understand and identify how a product fits into the buyer's value chain, in order to create the added value for the buyer (Porter, 1998, 2004).

Buyer Value

A firm creates value for a buyer that justifies a premium price (or preference at an equal price) through two mechanisms (Porter, 1998, 2004):

1. By lowering the buyer's cost.
2. By raising the buyer's performance.

If a firm is able to lower its buyer's cost or enhance its buyer's performance, it is likely that the buyer will be willing to pay a premium price. For example, a firm provides better after-sales services to its buyer that reduce both time and cost, and at the same time increases convenience to the buyer. Nevertheless, there are also many organizations which have other objectives which are not driven solely by profits or revenue growth; these should also be considered when analyzing the buyer's value chain.

Value Chain and Buyer's Value

A firm lowers the buyer's cost or raises the buyer's performance through the impact of its value chain on the buyer's value chain. A firm may affect the buyer's chain by simply providing an input to a single buyer's activity. The success depends on the relationship between a firm and its buyer's value chain that are relevant to the buyer's value, and on how the firm's product is actually used by the buyer. The more direct and indirect impacts a product has on its buyer's value chain, the richer would differentiation tends to be and thus the greater the overall level of achievable differentiation (Porter, 1998, 2004).

Lower Buyer's Cost

Anything a firm can do that lowers the buyer's total costs of using a product or other buyer's costs would represent a potential basis for differentiation. Actions that lower the costs of the buyer's value activities which represent a significant fraction of the buyer's costs would constitute the most significant opportunities (Porter, 1998, 2004).

Raising Buyer's Performance

Raising the buyer's performance would depend on understanding what desirable performance is from the buyer's viewpoint. In seeking for such opportunities, a firm must chart in details how its products can affect the buyer's value chain and administrative activities, so as to convince the buyer that the true value of raising the latter's product performance would benefit the buyer as a whole (Porter, 1998, 2004).

Buyer's Perception of Value

Buyers frequently do not fully understand the way in which a supplier actually or potentially might lower their costs or improve their performance. While buyers are more likely to perceive the direct impacts of a firm on their value chains, they often fall short of recognizing the indirect impacts in which other suppliers' activities, besides the product, could affect them. For instance, the buyer sometimes sees only the price of a product when measuring its value and do not add up other additional hidden costs. Firms can, for that reason, exploit the buyer's incomplete knowledge of what is valuable to the buyer and can therefore become an opportunity for implementing the differentiation strategy. This is because a firm may be able to adopt a new form of differentiation preemptively and educate the buyers to value its uniqueness (Porter, 1998, 2004).

Buyers will not pay for value that they do not perceive, no matter how real it is. Hence, the price premium a firm commands will therefore reflect both the value actually delivered to its buyer and the extent to which the buyer perceives this value as. In this context, the buyer goes through the three phases of perceived value, realized differentiation and actual value. The buyer would also compare between firms providing the desired service or product. For this purpose, the buyer would compare and consider the perceived value, realized differentiation and actual value for two or more suppliers. In the early stage, the buyer may for example consider the perceived value of Supplier B to be higher than that of Supplier A. This may change with time with the buyer eventually realizing that the actual value received from Supplier A is higher than that of Supplier B. Therefore in its failure to signal its value effectively across to the buyer, a firm may never be able to command the price premium its value actually deserves (Porter, 1998, 2004).

Buyer's Purchase Criteria

Applying the above-mentioned fundamentals of the buyer's value to a particular industry would result in the identification of the buyer's purchase criteria. Porter (1998, 2004) defined this as specific attributes of a firm that create actual or perceived value for the buyer. The buyer's purchase criteria can be divided into two categories; namely use criteria and signaling criteria. The price premium a firm can command will be a function of its uniqueness in fulfilling both the use and signaling criteria. With the purpose of determining an appropriate price premium, a firm must first understand how well it fulfils the use criteria as well as the value created for the buyer.

Use Criteria

The use criteria encompass the actual product or the system by which a firm delivers and supports its products, even if the physical product is undifferentiated. This includes the specifications achieved by a firm's product as well as the consistency with which it meets those specifications. It also includes intangibles such as style, prestige, perceived status and brand connotation (Porter, 1998, 2004).

Signaling Criteria

The signaling criteria are most important when buyers have a difficult time measuring a firm's performance. Consequently, the key strategy is to differentiate the company from rivals (Allen and Helms, 2006; Cheah and Garvin, 2004; Hill, 1988) through regular communications. A firm would have achieved its contribution if its buyers can often have a major impact on differentiation. Advertizing may emphasize product characteristics, while a firm's reputation may imply to some buyers that many of their criteria will be satisfied (Porter, 1998, 2004).

Identifying Purchase Criteria

The use criteria must be identified precisely in order to be meaningful for developing a differentiation strategy. Many firms speak of their buyers' use criteria in vague terms such as "high quality" or "delivery". At this level of generality, a firm cannot begin to calculate the value of meeting a use criterion to the buyer, nor can the firm know how to change its behavior to increase the buyer's value. The term "quality" is vague and can possibly mean anything from higher specifications to better conformance. Hence, good performance in satisfying each use criteria should be quantified (Porter, 1998, 2004), which the firm can then use to scrutinize the practices that underlie the performance of its competitors.

Like the use criteria, the signaling criteria should be defined as precisely and operationally as possible in order to guide the formulation of the differentiation strategy. In a bank, for example, the appearance of facilities can signal value through its order, permanence and security. The signaling criteria can vary in importance and a firm must rank these in terms of their impact on the buyer's perceptions in order for the firm to make choices over how much to spend on each of these criteria.

Differentiation Strategy

Differentiation stems from uniquely creating the buyer's value through satisfying the use or signaling criteria. Sustainable differentiation requires a firm to perform a range of value activities that impact these purchase criteria. Many value activities typically play a role in meeting some of the use or signaling criteria (Porter, 1998, 2004).

A successful differentiation strategy aims to create the largest gap between the buyer's value created (and hence the resulting price premium) and the cost of uniqueness in a firm's value chain. The costs of differentiation will vary by value activities and the firm should choose those activities where the contribution to the buyer's value is greatest relative to the costs. This may imply pursuing both low- and high-cost sources of uniqueness that have high buyer's value (Porter, 1998, 2004).

The final component of the differentiation strategy is sustainability. Differentiation will not lead to a premium price in the long run unless its sources remain valuable to the buyer and cannot be imitated by the competitors (Porter, 1998. 2004). Thus a firm must find durable sources of uniqueness that can withstand against the test of time from imitation.

Routes to Differentiation
Porter (1998, 2004) categorized differentiation in two basic ways. Firstly, a firm may become more unique in performing its existing value activities and secondly, it may reconfigure its value chain in some ways that enhance its

uniqueness. Becoming more unique in its value activities requires that a firm manipulates its drivers of uniqueness as described earlier. In both cases, a differentiator must simultaneously control the costs of differentiation so that it translates into superior performance (Porter, 1998, 2004).

Technology and Competitive Advantage

Technological change is one of the important determinants of competition. It has a major function in structural change in an industry as well as in creating new industries. Technology can also erode the competitive advantage of even well entrenched firms and drive others to the forefront. Of all the things that can change the rules of competition, technological change seems to be among the most prominent property for consideration.

Regardless of its importance, however, the relationship between technological change and competition is widely misunderstood. Technological change tends to be viewed as valuable for its own sake – any technological modification a firm can pioneer is believed to be good. Technological change, on the contrary, is not important for its own sake, but is important only if it affects competitive advantage and industry structure. However, Porter (1998, 2004) warned that not all technological change is strategically beneficial.

Technology and the Value Chain

The basic tool for understanding the function of technology in competitive advantage is the value chain. A firm, as a collection of activities, is basically composed of a collection of technologies (Porter, 1998, 2004). Technology is embodied in every value activity in a firm and technological change can affect competition through its impact on virtually any activity.

Technology and Competitive Advantage

Technology affects competitive advantage if it has a beneficial role in determining the relative cost position or differentiation. Technology will only influence costs or differentiation when cost drivers or drivers of uniqueness of value activities are affected. In addition, technology can impinge on competitive advantage through changing or influencing the other drivers of costs and uniqueness. Technological development can raise or lower scales of economies, make interrelationships possible, create the opportunity for advantages in timing and influence nearly any of the other drivers of costs or uniqueness. Thus, a firm can use technological development to alter drivers in a way that favors it, or to be the first and perhaps only firm to exploit a particular driver (Porter, 1998, 2004).

There is a misconception that technological development involves scientific breakthroughs or even technologies that were not widely available previously. Contrary to this viewpoint, technological development can also connote mundane changes in the way a firm performs activities or combines available technologies that often underlie competitive advantage.

Technology Strategy
The power of technological change can influence the industry structure and competitive advantage. For this reason, a firm's technological strategy then becomes a vital approach towards development. However, the use of technology must be taken within a broader perspective rather than limiting it to the role of research and development (R&D) because of the pervasive impact of technology on the entire value chain. Furthermore, technology strategy is only one element of the firm's overall competitive strategy and must be both consistent and reinforced by choices in other value activities (Porter, 1998, 2004).

Choice of Technologies to Develop
The technologies that should be developed are those that would contribute most to the firm's generic strategy. A firm should concentrate on technologies that have the greatest sustainable impact on costs or differentiation. The choice of technologies should not be limited only to those few where there are opportunities for major breakthroughs. In addition, Porter (1998, 2004) argued that modest improvements in several of the technologies in the value chain can add up to a greater benefit for competitive advantage due to the presence of linkages. Moreover, cumulative improvements in many activities can be more sustainable than a breakthrough that is noticeable to competitors and thereby becomes an easy target for imitation.

Imperfections of Generic Strategies

Porter (1998, 2004) proposed that cost advantage and differentiation are fundamentally two very different concepts in competitive advantage. For this reason, firms should only choose one of the two propositions. On the other hand, firms who choose the hybrid approach cannot achieve the same performance if they were to adopt just one strategic position. The failure to develop strategy in at least one of the two directions – a firm is said to be "stuck in the middle" in this scenario - would lead to an extremely poor strategic situation (almost doomed to failure). This is because the firm is almost guaranteed low profitability; it either loses the high volume customers who demand low prices or loses high-margin businesses to the firms who are focused in specific targets or have achieved overall differentiation (Porter, 1998, 2004). In spite of this, Porter (2004:18) highlighted that there are three exceptional conditions where a firm can simultaneously achieve both cost leadership and differentiation:

1. All competitors are stuck in the middle and that none is in any position to achieve any one of the generic strategies.
2. The cost position of firms are pretty much dependent on market share, rather than by the level of service provided, level of technology or other factors. At the same time, it occurs when there are important interrelationships that one competitor can take advantage of.
3. A firm breaks new grounds by pioneering a significant and innovative technology which can reap the benefits of both generic strategies.

On the contrary, further studies have shown that firms adopting the hybrid theory do not appear to face the precarious predicament which Porter (2004) had described (Miller and Dess, 1993; Miller, 1992). Contrary to Porter's (2004) findings, being stuck in the middle means firms with a blurred corporate culture are such that they focus on all generic strategies that it could well be argued that a "jack of all trades but master of none" strategy is being adopted (Miller and Dess, 1993). In reiteration, many other studies had found hybrid strategies (in certain industries) to be feasible where it was proven that these hybrid strategies can exhibit a higher performance over merely choosing either cost advantage or differentiation in isolation (Robert and O'Brien, 1998; Rugman and Verbeke, 1996; Dess and Miller, 1993). Similarly, Spanos, Zaralis and Lioukas (2004), Helms, Clay and Peter (1997) and Hill (1988) found that businesses which simultaneously compete on the low cost and differentiation combination can also be equally successful. This suggests that the two strategies can co-exist. Wright, et al (1991) has identified successful firms using combined generic strategies in industries such as banking, retailing, distributing and creative businesses. With this in mind, Miller (1992:41) suggested a few scenarios where hybrid strategies may thrive:

1. When buyers have more than one priority about the product (e.g. price, quality, style and features).
2. When it is easy for competitors to mimic pure strategies.
3. When there is no conflict between two strategies.
4. When rivals become too narrowly focused around a single aspect of strategy and require more openness.
5. Where differentiation by innovative products or low costs by more economic processes or both are difficult to achieve.

Chapter 4

OBSERVATIONS IN CONSTRUCTION FIRMS

INTRODUCTION

The construction market is different from the conventional markets; the latter indicates that a market exists where the buyers and sellers of a homogenous product are in sufficiently close contact with one another such that a single price prevails (Ngowi, Iwisi and Mushi, 2002; Ofori, 2002; Kim, 1997; Honer and Zakieh, 1996). However, it is unclear whether this strict definition of a market can be applied within the context of the construction industry because in reality, there is generally no homogenous product or service with a single price in the construction market.

INDUSTRY INSTABILITY AND COMPETITIVE WARFARE

In most industries, a central characteristic of competition is that firms are mutually dependent; firms feel the effects of each others' strategic moves and are prone to react to them. The first question for the firm in considering offensive or defensive moves is the general degree of instability in the industry or the industry-wide conditions that may mean a move will touch off aggressive competition. The underlying structure of an industry, discussed earlier in Chapter 2, determines the intensity of competitive rivalry and the general ease or difficulty that cooperative or warfare-avoiding outcomes can be found. Industry structure influences the position of the competitors, the pressures on them to make aggressive moves and the degree to which their interests are likely to conflict. Structure thus sets the basic parameters within which competitive moves are made (Porter, 1998, 2004).

In the context of the construction industry in Singapore, at the time of this study, there were 57 Grade Al and Grade A2 general contractors who have commonly been described to be the larger contractors. These general contractors are registered with Singapore's Building and Construction Authority with a view to bidding for public sector building projects. The Grade A1 general contractors, for example, can bid for building projects with unlimited tendering capabilities. For reason of their size, the Grade A1 and Grade A2 general contractors in Singapore generally share the same conventional wisdom about who their customers are, how they generate value and what the scope of products and services their industry should be offering. The more these construction firms compete along similar paths, the more rigorous the rivalry is likely to be. Fierce competition based on such activities alone is mutually destructive, leading to endless price wars – sometimes lower than the owner's budget (Lo, Lin and Yan, 2007). This may consequently lead to zero-sum (competing away potential profits) competitive, static or declining prices and pressure on costs will continuously spiral downwards. As a result, this may compromise on the companies' ability to invest in the business for the long run. This is in stark contrast for firms who target distinct customer segments i.e. different types of customers; where the effect on each other appears to be less severe.

DEFINITION OF STRATEGY AND BEHAVIOR

As noted by Johnson and Scholes (1999:10), "Strategy is the direction and scope of an organization over the long term; which achieves competitive advantage for the organization through its configuration of resources within a changing environment, to meet the needs of markets and to fulfill stakeholder expectations." By using an effective competitive strategy, a company can find its niche and learn more about its clients (Porter, 1981). Porter (1996, 2004) emphasized that there are three basic business strategies – differentiation, cost leadership and focus – and a company performs best by choosing only one out of the three strategies. However, other researchers (Hlavacka et al, 2001; Fuerer and Chaharbaghi, 1997) felt that a combination of these strategies may offer a company a better chance to achieve competitive advantage. While various types of competitive strategies have been identified over the past decade (Porter, 1981, 1996), Porter (2004) suggested that in order to sustain long term profitability, the firm must choose between the three generic strategies rather being "stuck in the middle".

COMPETITIVE STRATEGY IN CONSTRUCTION

This section sets out the analytical foundation for the development of competitive strategy, built on the analysis of the construction industry structure and competitors by incorporating the concept of structural analysis as a framework for understanding the five structural forces of competitive advantage in the construction industry in Singapore.

Threat of Entry

Product Differentiation

In this context, established firms have brand identification and customer loyalties that are accumulated from past building projects resulting in product differentiation. Hence, in order for new entrants to enter, this effort would usually involve start-up losses and often takes an extended period of time to accomplish. For instance, many European construction firms have tried to establish their base in Singapore but, apart from a few, were generally unsuccessful in doing so (Low, 1996).

Capital Requirements

The need to invest large financial resources in order to compete creates a barrier to entry. In this context, construction projects usually rake up millions of dollars in investments and are usually unrecoverable until the end of the project, particularly if the projects had suffered a loss.

Proprietary Product Technology

In this context, firms in the local market would have acquired the product know-how or design characteristics that are kept proprietary through secrecy and confidential cover.

Experience and Scale as Entry Barriers

The presence of economies of scale always leads to a cost advantage for larger firms over the smaller ones. This is assuming that the former have efficient facilities, distribution systems and other functional activities. The large firms are then able to spread the fixed costs of operating these facilities over a large scale project or multiple small projects whereas the smaller firms, even if they have technologically efficient facilities will not be able to fully utilize them.

Intensity of Rivalry among Existing Competitors

Pricing in the Singapore construction industry is by far oriented towards costs, with the norms of deriving detailed costs of quantities for the building elements and then applying a mark up based on the company's preference or gut feel (Low and Teo, 2005). On the same note, buyers understandably have the propensity to accept the lowest bids submitted by the various interested firms because of the huge sums of money involved in constructing the physical facilities. Consequently, in order to secure jobs, contractors engaged in price competition with each other.

High Fixed or Storage Costs
High fixed costs arising from capital investments in heavy equipment such as cranes and excavators can create strong pressures for contractors to fill capacity which often lead to rapidly escalating price cutting when equipment are left idle.

Lack of Differentiation or Switching Costs
Likewise, where the product is perceived as a commodity, the developer would place price as a first priority, and pressure for the most competitive price would inevitably result.

Pressure from Substitute Products

The uniqueness about the construction industry is that there is hardly any choice for substitute products. There are no alternatives to replace what is required by the client.

Bargaining Power of Buyers

As mentioned earlier, clients often play a key role in driving the project costs down, leaving minimum profits for the contractors. Contractors are not in a position to command premium prices as the buyers themselves are too price sensitive because of the following reasons:

1. The huge portion, usually the entire project, is purchased by a given developer. This raises the importance of the buyer's business to the contractors.
2. Developers are confident that they can always find alternative contractors for their projects.
3. The developers have full information about the various tender bids submitted by the contractors and would also have some knowledge of the contractors' mark-up prices.
4. There is no penalty for product failure for the developers as contractors are expected to comply with specifications and make good all defects during the defects liability period.

Bargaining Power of Suppliers

Due to the general abundance of suppliers in the marketplace, suppliers are now placed in the contractor's shoes as they are dependent on the contractor's orders for sustaining their businesses. All or most contractors would source for the lowest price for their resources whether for the same quality or something less superior.

GENERIC COMPETITIVE STRATEGIES

Cost Leadership

All firms in the low cost strategy who submit a competitive bid would want to achieve the lowest possible operation cost in order to be awarded the project. Porter (1998, 2004) observed that having a cost leadership would mean that firms can earn a healthy margin by protecting themselves from the five competitive forces, as compared to their rivals who have competed away from their profits through rivalry where the less efficient competitors will suffer first in the face of competitive pressures.

Differentiation

Firms create something that is perceived industry-wide as being unique. Hence Porter (1998, 2004) suggested a number of approaches to differentiation that can take many forms: brand image, technology pioneer, quality buildings, environmentally conscious contractors and other dimensions (Porter, 1998, 2004). Differentiation provides insulation against competitive rivalry because of the uniqueness that the firm has set itself apart from its rivals, thus resulting in lower sensitivity to price (Lo, Lin and Yan, 2007). For that reason, this would be a viable strategy for earning above-average returns as it creates a defensible position for coping with the five competitive forces, albeit in a different way than cost leadership. An example of this scenario would be through the buyer's loyalty to the firm that translates to the willingness to pay a high price for the services rendered (Hlavacka et al, 2001; Fuerer and Chaharbaghi, 1997). For instance, clients can enter into a negotiated mode of procurement with the main contractor, doing away with the traditional competitive mode of procurement.

Focus

Firms in this specific segment focused on a particular buyer group, type of buildings, service line or geographical markets (Ming, Runeson and Skitmore, 1996; Rwelamila, 2002; Seaden, et al, 2003). Although the low cost and differentiation strategies are aimed at achieving their objectives industry-wide, the focus strategy is built around contractors who aim to serve a particular market, i.e. in the public or private sector, commercial, residential or industrial segment. With such a narrow strategic target, firms serve this segment more effectively and efficiently than competitors who are competing broadly. As a result, firms achieve either differentiation from better meeting the needs of the particular target or lower costs in serving this target (Porter, 1998, 2004).

Stuck in the Middle

Unfortunately, not all firms have a distinctive strategic position and most of them are likely to be found vaguely in either the cost advantage segment or the precarious situation of getting caught in the middle. Consequently, without a defined strategic behavior, Porter (1998, 2004) suggested that such a firm is likely to be weeded out of the industry due to its inability to achieve low cost or attain a unique position in the industry.

BUYERS AND SUPPLIERS

Price Sensitivity of Buyers

The Buyer is very Profitable and Can Readily Pass on the Cost of Inputs
Highly profitable buyers tend to be less price sensitive than those in marginal financial conditions. Firms can target these buyers with above market rates through effective use and signal criteria, to successfully signal its value to the buyers.

The Buyer Seeks a Customized Design or Differentiated Variety
If the property developer wants a specially designed building which involves complex construction operations, then this desire would often be compensated by a premium price for the project costs. This situation can apply to specialist firms who have such expertise in delivering the exact client's requirements. In this context, such contractors will have more bargaining power over the costs of the project than others.

Purchasing Strategy

Spread Purchases
Contractors do not usually limit their purchases to just one supplier and one subcontractor; instead purchasing is spread among a pool of suitable suppliers and subcontractors to improve their bargaining position. However, it is important not to spread the purchases too widely so much so that this does not take advantage of discounts on bulk purchasing.

Sourcing for Alternate Sources
Firms have been found to be using repeated materials for their building projects. Instead they should be more proactive to source for alternative materials to bring about more value to the buyer's value chain. For example, a higher quality and more expensive material can give a longer life span to the building and reduce the need for more frequent maintenance.

Structural Analysis

Strategic Groups

In the construction industry in Singapore, the larger Grade A1 and Grade A2 general contractors seem to adopt similar strategic approaches. This can be seen when they are affected to a large extent by similar events in the industry and appear to have adopted similar responses to such external events or competitive moves. Nevertheless, this should not be confused with the abilities of these firms to implement the common strategy. This is where actual profitability is realized between one who promises to deliver with another who actually delivers.

Mobility Barriers

Mobility barriers form the first major reason why some firms are more profitable than others, those that have high mobility barriers as compared to those with low mobility barriers. Without mobility barriers, contractors with successful strategies will be imitated such as those who initially enjoyed a low cost position, say hiring low cost laborers. They would find their positions being eroded easily as other rivals are able to quickly imitate through better execution (Porter, 1998, 2004). Hence, it is recommended that contractors invest in high mobility barriers that disallow easy imitation or duplication, bearing in mind to some extent that the firm would need to trade short-term profitability for long-term profitability.

Bargaining Power

The bargaining power contractors have with suppliers is very much dependent on the volume of purchases, such that the larger construction firms would command greater bargaining power with suppliers relative to the smaller construction firms.

Rivalry among Firms

An important influence on rivalry is the market interdependence of contractors – the degree that the contractors are competing for the same buyers (private or public buyers), for example, firms who respond to a specific tender are all vying for the same project. Moreover, in the construction industry in Singapore, between the larger Grade A1 and Grade A2 general contractors, they are rather similar in size and capability that there is a high probability that if one firm is to succumb to submit a penetration bid then it is likely that the rest will follow suit. In penetration bidding, contractors submit abnormally low bids,

.eeping the profit margin deliberately low and consistently lower than the market .iorms, while hoping to break even or to profit during the project phase from cutting corners to reduce costs or raising claims against the client (Crowley and Hancher, 1995). From the above, it can be observed that the marketplace situation in the construction industry in Singapore can be extremely volatile.

Firm's Profitability

Not all contractors pursuing the same strategy will necessarily be profitable, the main reason being that some contractors are more superior in their abilities to coordinate and manage operations, make technological breakthroughs, develop creative ideas and so on. As one would expect, contractors with superior implementation abilities will be more profitable than other firms in the same strategic group.

COMPETITIVE ADVANTAGE IN CONSTRUCTION

The theory behind competitive advantage is an activity-based theory of the firm that seeks to provide a general framework for thinking strategically about the activities involved in any business and assessing their relative costs and role in differentiation.

Primary Activities in the Value Chain

As noted earlier, there are five generic categories of primary activities in competing in any industry.

Inbound Logistics

Inbound logistics are activities associated with receiving, storing and disseminating inputs in the building project such as handling, inventory control and vehicle scheduling. These are essential to keep activities on site as efficient as possible without excessive inventory that will pose problems in a congested site (Koskela, 1992).

Operations

Operations are activities associated with transforming inputs into the final building product such as construction of the facility itself (assembly), maintenance, testing and commissioning, and facility operations.

Outbound Logistics

Outbound logistics are activities associated with collecting, storing and physically distributing the product to buyers, such as finished goods warehousing, material handling, delivery vehicle operations and scheduling.

Marketing and Sales

These are activities associated with providing avenues by which buyers i.e. developers can purchase the product and inducing them to do so through aggressive advertising, promotion, sales force and pricing. What is unique in the construction industry is that it is unheard of for contractors to induce demand; it appears that they are not able to construct a facility before the demand of the buyer has been made known (Cheah and Garvin, 2004; Porter, 2004).

Service

These are activities associated with providing service to enhance or maintain the value of the product such as the construction activities – installation, repair, training and product adjustment.

Support Value Activities

Likewise, support value activities involved in competing in any industry can be divided into four generic categories, as discussed below.

Procurement

This refers to the function of purchasing inputs used in the firm's value chain and not to the purchased inputs themselves (Porter, 1998, 2004). Material costs such as raw materials and plants usually form the bulk of the construction costs of any projects. Not surprisingly, firms conscientiously source for the lowest price possible among the suppliers and subcontractors (Sacks and Harel, 2006; Low and Leong, 2001). Inevitably, firms usually emphasize on bulky commodities such as concrete and equipment which seem to be the best possible areas to cut costs. Unfortunately, the costs of procurement activities themselves usually represent an insignificant portion of total costs, but often have a large impact on the firm's overall costs and differentiation (Porter, 1998, 2004). Improving purchasing practices can strongly affect the costs and even quality of the purchased inputs. Adding on, Rahman and Kumaraswamy (2004) observed that partnering between the main contractors and subcontractors is habitually on a project basis rather than long term partnering. Such behavior only encourages short term opportunistic behavior but limits long term performance for both parties such as maximizing the effectiveness of resources and active search for continuous improvements (Bennett and Jayes, 1995).

Technology Development

Technology pervades in every value activity which consists of a wide range of activities that can be attributed to improve not only the end product but also the processes. Despite the fact that technology can help to improve the position of the firms, the construction industry in Singapore appears to adamantly utilize minimal technology which still reflects labor intensive practices. This is because of the cheap source of foreign workers which is readily available in the construction industry.

Human Resource Management

Employees form the backbone of any firm whereby they support and carry out the firm's day-to-day business operations and possibly search for new ventures through upgrading of employee skills/knowledge, hiring experienced workers and hiring well-trained new graduates (Cheah and Garvin, 2004; Seaden et al, 2003).

COST ADVANTAGE

Cost advantage is one of the two types of competitive advantage that a firm may choose to compete with. A number of firms have the tendency to take on the factor of cost down to a few narrow issues, usually resorting to simplistic comparisons of labor rates and raw materials. The absence of a systematic framework prohibits the study of individual activities being analyzed sequentially, ignoring the linkages among activities that can potentially offer cost savings (Porter, 2004).

Cost Drivers

In this context, cost drivers are the main determinants of cost. For this reason, major cost drivers that determine the cost behavior of value activities of construction firms are described below.

Economies or Diseconomies of Scale

Firms working on building projects try to achieve economies of scale by making sure that they are more efficient at full capacity on a large scale. This is especially relevant to those who own proprietary technology that makes it economical for them to handle larger scale projects so as to take advantage of economies of scale. The advantage of economies of scale is not limited just to operating on large scale projects; it can take place in virtually every value activity in a firm.

Learning and Spillovers

Working from one project to another allow firms to accumulate the experience and thus steepening the learning curve each time with further reduction in costs (Ghemawat, 1985) such as layout changes, improved scheduling, labor efficiency improvement and project design modifications which facilitate the increased utilization of assets and better tailoring of raw materials to the process. Hence, learning is built up through cumulative experience and "learning by doing". In addition, Knuf (2002) had noted that benchmarking helps to formulate a framework that is deemed to be the best in practice.

Linkages

It has long been recognized that 80 percent of the value of a bill of quantities in the construction industry is contained in only 20 percent of the items (Ashworth and Skitmore, 1983). Hence, firms place their attention on the 20 percent worth of items towards estimating and controlling the costs of construction projects. However, examining cost behavior through the 20 percent of items alone is surely inadequate, as it fails to identify integration of other linkages that have the possibilities to lower the total costs.

Timing

The cost of a value activity often reflects timing. Sometimes a firm may gain a first-mover advantage from being the pioneering firm to take a particular action but late-movers can also enjoy benefits and yet avoid high product or market development capital costs. So far, many contractors in Singapore do not appear to be known for capitalizing on their first-mover advantage (Low and Lim, 1999).

Discretionary Policies Independent of other Drivers

The cost of a value activity is always affected by policy choices a firm makes, often quite independent of other cost drivers. This reflects the contractor's strategy between cost advantage and differentiation. Some of the policy choices that tend to have the greatest impact on cost include:

1. Product configuration and performance.
2. Process technology chosen.
3. The specifications of raw materials or other purchased inputs used (e.g. raw materials quality affects the final product).
4. Wages paid and amenities provided to employees.
5. Procedures for scheduling production, maintenance, the sales force and other activities.

Cost Dynamics

The concept of cost dynamics enables early identification, thereby allowing a firm to forecast how the cost drivers may vary and which value activities will increase or decrease in absolute or relative cost importance, in respect of today's fast moving economy – as a firm grows or as industry conditions change (Porter, 1998, 2004).

Industry's Real Growth

In recent years, and before the onslaught of the global economic crisis that began in 2008 in the United States, Singapore appears to ride on the waves of worldwide economic prosperity and growth. This brings good news to many industries but in the construction industry, growth increases the costs of purchased inputs by upsetting the supply and demand equilibrium.

Relative Inflation of Costs

The rate of inflation in key cost elements in value activities can significantly shift their relative costs that challenge contractors to execute strategic decisions to overcome the inflated materials prices.

GAINING COST ADVANTAGE

There are two major ways that contractors can gain a cost advantage, either to control cost drivers or reconfigure the value chain. These two sources are not mutually exclusive. Successful cost advantages derive from numerous sources within the value chain and require a careful examination of every activities in a firm for opportunities to reduce costs and most importantly, the consistent pursuit of all of them (Porter, 1998, 2004).

Control Cost Drivers

A firm can gain an advantage with respect to the cost drivers of value activities representing a significant proportion of total costs.

Gaining the Appropriate Type of Scale

Contractors can increase their scale through acquisitions, product line extensions or market expansion to lower their costs. This might be appropriate for contractors to expand their operations during favorable economic climate (Low, 1992).

Emphasize Value Activities Driven by Types of Scale where the Firm Has an Advantage

Firms should set their strategies to emphasize their economies of scale as much as possible the activities in which they have superior scale of the appropriate type. On the other hand, firms who have scarce resources should not try to imitate large firms who have the capabilities to build and create large quantities of resources (Ngowi, Iwisi and Mushi, 2002).

Management with the Learning Curve and Keep Learning Exclusive

The turnover rate for employees can be high, especially during the good times, when they are lured by the high wages offered by rival companies. Besides this, contractors are not able to retain their employees because of the lack of investments in upgrading their employees. Firms must realize that learning does not occur automatically but results from the efforts and attention of both management and employees.

Learn from Competitors

There is a lack of a proper avenue for contractors to learn from each other, studying published materials and articles about competitors not only locally but also globally, in order to avail the firm to uncover good ideas that can be applied in-house. In addition, contractors work in some level of secrecy and confidential cover that would make it extremely difficult for them to share information with other stakeholders in the construction industry.

Exploit Cost Linkages within the Value Chain

Contractors can enhance their cost positions if they are able to recognize linkages among value activities and exploit them. In this context, an appropriate choice of building materials or construction methods can help to enhance the linkages within the value chain. Furthermore, the speed of recent technological advances had made information communication easier, making coordination work among activities readily achievable (Porter, 1998, 2004).

Work with Subcontractors and Channels to Exploit Vertical Linkages

Vertical linkages are recommended as these can offer possibilities for the various subcontractors to work together by systematic coordination and proper communication through long term alliances (Low, 1992; Low and Lim, 1999). In order for this to succeed, there must be determination to overcome suspicion and greed. The main contractor must be prepared, to be open to share the gains of linkages with the subcontractors (Porter, 1998, 2004).

Time Purchases in the Business Cycle

Purchasing assets during periods of weak demand can yield major cost savings. This is the case for many capital goods such as machinery, land and even completed buildings.

Invest in Technology to Skew Cost Drivers in the Firm's Favor

New technology often underlies the cost advantage that contractors benefit from by developing low cost processes in the long term. This is clearly demonstrated in the Japanese construction firms who spent about 3 percent of their gross receipts in technology development, the highest R&D spending in the construction sector (Raftery et al, 1998). Still, contractors do not seem to be investing aggressively enough in new technologies due to the initially high paid up capital and the risk of not being able to reap the benefits even after making the investments (Sexton, Barrett and Aouad, 2006).

Enhanced Bargaining Leverage through Purchasing Policies

As mentioned earlier, procurement can prove to be an essential tool that affects costs. Hence, contractors can enhance their bargaining power with suppliers by undertaking a number of specific actions:

1. Not to be over-reliant with one supplier, but keep the number of sources sufficient to ensure competition.
2. Select suppliers who are especially competitive with each other and divide the purchases among them.
3. Appoint high-quality purchasing executives to allow more sophisticated buying practices.

Select Appropriate Suppliers and Manage their Costs

Contractors select suppliers whom they can form long term partnerships with, such as pre-bid agreements, to ensure quality assurance and competitive bids for the buyers.

Reconfigure the Value Chain

Dramatic shifts in the relative cost position can be attained through adopting a value chain that is significantly different from its own and their competitors. Such reconfiguration can stem from a number of sources such as:

1. A different production process
2. A new raw material
3. A new distribution channel
4. A new advertising media

Cost Advantage through Focus

A focus strategy, derived from employing a different and customized value chain to serve the specific target segment allows contractors to channel their efforts to a well-chosen segment of an industry that can often lower costs significantly. Some contractors may base their strategy in the private residential segment only, while others may direct theirs in the domain of public infrastructural works.

DIFFERENTIATION

The differentiation strategy is all about creating an edge that sets one contractor apart on the notion of "uniqueness" in order to appeal to the clients (Allen and Helms, 2006). This begs the question of how different the contractors are. Are they differentiated or just different?

Differentiation and Value Chain

Differentiation can take place and potentially contribute in any activity in the value chain along the same line as Porter's (1981, 1996) value system concept. In this context, construction projects can likewise create new value for the clients through the primary activities and the support activities. The representative sources of differentiation in the value chain of a construction firm in the primary activities would include the following (Porter, 1998, 2004):

1. Inbound logistics – dealing with handling of inputs that minimizes damages, etc.
2. Operations – dealing with strict conformance to specifications, attractive building appearance, being responsive to changes in specifications, low rates of defects, etc.
3. Outbound logistics – dealing with rapid and timely deliveries, production that minimizes damages, etc.
4. Marketing and sales – dealing with high reputation, personal relationships with suppliers and buyers, etc.
5. Service – dealing with rapid production and installation, high service quality, etc.

The representative sources of differentiation in the value chain of a construction firm in the support activities would include the following, including integration with the respective primary activities being shown in brackets (Porter, 1998, 2004):

1. Infrastructure of the firm – involving top management support in selling facilities that enhance the firm's image (across all five primary activities of Inbound logistics, Operations, Outbound logistics, Marketing and sales, and Service).

2. Human resource management – dealing with the superior training of personnel (Inbound logistics); programs to attract talents (Operations); sales and service personnel (Marketing and sales); and extensive training (Service).
3. Technology development – dealing with superior material handling (Inbound logistics); unique product features and unique product processes (Operations); unique scheduling (Outbound logistics); superior market research (Marketing and sales); and advanced servicing techniques (Service).
4. Procurement – dealing with the highest quality raw materials and components (Operations); location of raw supplies (Outbound logistics); product image (Marketing and sales); and high after-sales quality (Service).

Procurement

The procurement of raw materials and other inputs can affect the performance and quality of the building when this is being customized to meet the client's needs. This can create a position of differentiation for the contractor.

Primary and Support Activities

Operational activities can affect the uniqueness in the design of the building, product appearance and quality. All these are done to improve the net worth to the client in terms of shortening the construction period, enhancing safety, attaining environmentally friendly goals or improve the quality of the building (Mahmoud-Jouini, 2000).

Indirect Activities

It is arguable that construction is essentially about providing a service to the owners rather than the product itself because construction is a multi-faceted coordination process involving the main contractor, client, consultants, subcontractors and suppliers. It is a norm for subcontract works to account for up to 80 percent of the costs of most projects, involving the suppliers, trades subcontractors and labor only subcontractors. This is over and above the need to harmonize and coordinate the various building services engineering, architectural and structural works with the architects, engineers and other consultants (Macomber, 1989).

Drivers of Uniqueness

There are causal reasons why an activity is unique; identifying them allows contractors to fully develop their new forms of differentiation or examine the extent of how sustainable their existing differentiation is.

Policy Choices

This is perhaps the single most prevalent driver that firms make policy choices about what activities to perform and how to perform them. Hence, there is a mandatory need for the top management of the firm to formulate an appropriate strategy and remain committed to steer the policy drivers towards differentiation.

Product features and Performance Offered

Contractors offer services other than general contracting activities, such as design, engineering, project financing and project management activities (Whitla, Walters and Davies, 2006) in order to create a package that gives the maximum value to the client. This is especially so through the design and build procurement mode which can realize the full potential of the contractors as they are given the full reign of conceptualizing the projects through the client's design briefs (Mahmoud-Jouini, 2000).

Technology Employed in Performing an Activity

Larger construction firms have greater levels of resources that allow them to engage in more or wider variety of innovations, while the smaller firms tend to be less innovative (Seaden et al, 2003). By fostering innovation and creativity as well as building a reputation of being technologically advanced, the firm is assured of meeting the interests of the new clients as well as catering to the existing client's demands for uniqueness (Allen and Helms, 2006). Allen and Helms (2006) suggested that innovation seemed to be the most vital factor for success.

Quality of Inputs Procured for an Activity

The better quality the materials are, the more costly these would be. Consequently, this may affect the budget of the contractors. Many of them are frequently too short-sighted, seeing the initial high costs while ignoring the potential huge savings that could be achieved along the value chains for both the contractor and the client.

Linkages

Within the Value Chain

Meeting the needs of the clients often involved linked activities, rather than just relying on a single value activity. Contractors would have achieved dramatic reductions in defect rates by modifying every activity that influences defects instead of just relying on the inspection stage of the project where rectification is by then inevitable.

Supplier Linkages

This is due to the result of close coordination with suppliers, where they can shorten new model development time as well as cutting back on delivery times especially for contractors who adopt the just-in-time mode for the procurement of materials (Low and Chan, 1997).

Interrelationships

Contractors enhance their uniqueness by capitalizing on their parent's business units through centralized activities and work extensively with intranets which pool knowledge and resources within the organization (Porter, 1998, 2004).

Integration

Integration into new value activities can make a firm unique because the firm is better able to control the performance of the activities or coordinate them with other activities (Low and Teo, 2005). Hence, a construction firm can undertake a cluster of similar activities instead of sub-packaging these to the subcontractors to foster closer integration.

Scale

Large scale can allow an activity to be performed in a unique way that is not possible at smaller scale. In some cases, scale can work against the uniqueness of an activity. Scale may, for example, reduce the flexibility of niche construction firms to meet the client's needs (Porter, 1998, 2004).

Buyer's Purchase Criteria

Use Criteria

This encompasses the actual product by which the contractor delivers and supports its product through the quality of work, product and reputation to tremendously improve the clients' perceptions of them (Low, 1992; Mahmoud-Jouini, 2000).

Signaling Criteria

This reflects the signals of value that influence the client's perceptions of the contractor's ability to meet the intended use criteria especially when the former may face a hard time measuring the contractor's performance. This is because most construction firms in the same strategic group are deemed to have similar capacity and ability to deliver the final product. In addition, there are also some cases whereby building specifications are so precise that there is limited room for firms to propose alternatives or replacements. Typical signaling criteria include (Porter, 1998, 2004):

1. Reputation or image
2. Cumulative advertising
3. Packaging and labels
4. Time in business
5. Customer list
6. Market share
7. Price (where price connotes quality)
8. Parent company identity (size, financial stability, etc)

Buyer's Value

Lowering Buyer's Cost

Construction firms time and again appear to have a poor understanding of how their clients use the buildings. Otherwise, they can lower the client's total costs if they have a sophisticated understanding of how buyers use the products and how their various activities can affect the clients' costs (Porter, 1998, 2004). Pricing has thus far been too cost oriented, keeping the profit margin deliberately lower than the market standard in order to outbid competitors.

Raising Buyer's Performance

This is also commonly known as skimming where a contractor has to price relatively higher than the figure the market would allow, based on the belief that the company enjoys competitive advantage over the other bidders in terms of the client's crucial requirements and providing the latter with the best value (Lo, Lin and Yan, 2007). Hence, the better known the client's characteristics are, the higher would the bid be. By applying the proposed bidding process, clients also get to enjoy the best price in return for the most suitable contractor for their projects.

Sustainability of Differentiation

The degree of sustainability will vary from firms to firms. This depends on the vulnerability of the sources of differentiation and whether rivals are able to match up to their differentiation tactics.

Firm's Sources of Uniqueness Involving Barriers

Proprietary learning, linkages and interrelationships tend to be more sustainable drivers of uniqueness.

Sources of Differentiation Are Multiple

Contractors may find it hard to sustain their differentiation strategies as their strategies could stem from one single factor such as product quality or strict cost control practices. A single focal point would direct competitor's attention to just that one point, whereas differentiation from coordinated multiple integration and linkages can prove to be less imitable (Porter, 1998, 2004).

TECHNOLOGY AND COMPETITIVE ADVANTAGE

The fragmented nature of the construction industry in Singapore, in general, is one of the main reasons that caused firms to under-utilize the existing technology infrastructure, resources and government assistance schemes and incentives, in comparison to other developed countries, notably Japan where construction firms have invested heavily in research and development, the latest info-communication technology and heavy plant and equipment (Dulaimi et al, 2002). Technology can help construction firms create and/or deepen their competitive advantage, particularly so in the modern-world of today where information and communication technology are the pillars of the knowledge-based economy. Hence, how companies exploit and use these technologies holds the key to their performance in the market. It is said that technology increases with size; large construction firms have the tendency to use three times as many advanced technology as smaller construction firms (Seaden et al, 2003).

TECHNOLOGY IN THE VALUE CHAIN

Most firms appear to fear the word "technology" as they often associate it with breakthroughs and highly innovative technological systems. On the contrary, technology had made its position to exist in every value activities (in the firm's infrastructure, human resource management, technology development and procurement) in order to produce some outputs which take the forms of communication, plant and equipment, materials, systems, designs, business practices, quality and organization (Seaden et al, 2003; Gann, 1996). The effect is not limited to the firm's inward operations but also addresses the issue of fragmentation of the construction industry where through the use of technology, the introduction and adoption of the new procurement systems like design and build is made possible (Dulaimi et al, 2002).

In the foreseeable future when technology is pervasive enough, more varied forms of procurement systems could be introduced into the industry. It is recognized that technology may give rise to greater fragmentation in the industry. But this may not necessarily evolved to become a problem. This is because this pathway could in turn promote more healthy competition among firms wherein they are able to find their own niche areas in the different procurement systems instead of competing in the same domain as is the case today.

The representative sources of differentiating technology in the value chain of a construction firm in the primary activities would include the following (Porter, 1998, 2004):

1. Inbound logistics – dealing with transport technology, material handling, technology *per se,* and communication system technology, etc.
2. Operations – dealing with basic process technology, testing technology, building design/operation technology, and information system technology, etc.
3. Outbound logistics – dealing with transportation technology, and communication system technology, etc.

4.   Marketing and sales – dealing with communication system technology, and information system technology, etc.
5.   Service – dealing with diagnostic and testing technology, communication system technology, and information system technology, etc.

The representative sources of differentiating technology in the value chain of a construction firm in the support activities would include the following, including integration with the respective primary activities being shown in brackets (Porter, 1998, 2004):

1.   Infrastructure of the firm – involving information system technology, planning and budgeting technology, and office technology, etc. (across all five primary activities of Inbound logistics, Operations, Outbound logistics, Marketing and sales, and Service).
2.   Human resource management – involving training technology, and information system technology, etc. (Operations, Outbound logistics and Marketing and sales).
3.   Technology development – involving product technology, computer aided design, software development tools, and information system technology, etc. (Operations, Outbound logistics and Marketing and sales).
4.   Procurement – involving information system technology, computer system technology, and transport system technology, etc. (Operations, Outbound logistics and Marketing and sales).

RELATIONSHIP BETWEEN TECHNOLOGY AND COMPETITIVE ADVANTAGE

The relationship between technology and competitive advantage is that it can either help contractors to reduce costs or set them apart from their rivals on being unique.

Technological Change Lowers Cost or Enhances Differentiation and the Firm's Technological Lead is Sustainable

Many contractors do not invest enough in technology as the benefits cannot be realized during the short run and they do so without realizing that technology indeed has the potential to help them reduce costs or to be unique in the construction industry. Nevertheless, this pathway can offer them the opportunity to be more profitable longer than expected, particularly if the technology is hard to imitate or duplicate.

Technology and Rivalry

Technology can alter the nature and basis of rivalry among existing competitors in several ways. It can dramatically alter the cost structure and hence affect pricing decisions of construction firms (Porter, 1998, 2004). For instance, technology development had enabled construction firms to move away from the cost strategic groups into differentiation or focus strategy groups which can relieve the heat from intensive price competitions. In this context, the design and build procurement mode can help to ensure proper coordination between multiple parties and in the process, enhance the sourcing for engineering solutions and materials, among others.

Technological Change and Industry Attractiveness

It is sometimes believed that technological change always improves industry structure through the creation of varying intensities of healthy competition. However, the previous discussion had also highlighted that it is as likely to worsen industry structure as well. Nonetheless, the effect on this would depend on the nature of its impact on the five forces. If it gives the individual contractor more bargaining power due to the different technology that each uses (i.e. reduces the buyer's power), then this can improve industry profits (Porter, 1998, 2004).

Choices of Technologies to Develop

The technologies adopted should contribute most to a contractor's generic strategy; from cost leadership, differentiation and focus through either product technological change or process technological change (Porter, 1998, 2004).

Within the context of product technological change, the approaches can take the forms of:

1. Cost leadership – through product development to reduce product cost by lowering material contents and facilitating ease of manufacture or cost effective structural and building designs.
2. Differentiation – through product development to enhance product quality, features and deliverability.

3. Cost focus – through product development to design in only enough performance to meet the needs of the target segment.
4. Focus – through product design to meet the needs of a particular segment better than broadly-targeted competitors.

Within the context of process technological change, the approaches can likewise take the following forms:

1. Cost leadership – through (a) improving the learning curve process and reducing production usage or labor inputs; and (b) process development to enhance economies of scale.
2. Differentiation – through process development to support high tolerances, greater quality control and more reliable scheduling to tune the value chain for faster response time and other attributes that increase the buyer's value.
3. Cost focus – through process development to tune the value chain to serve and meet the needs of a low cost segment.
4. Focus – through process development to tune the value chain to meet the needs of a segment in order to raise the buyer's value.

Technological Fellowship

Arising from the perceived risks, contractors in Singapore do not appear to be active in leading technological innovations and processes; they also do not have their own R&D department to constantly explore for breakthroughs (Construction 21 Steering Committee, 1999). This could be due to the associated high costs of inputs such as raw materials, service facilities, training and the time needed for such developmental works. Contractors seem to lack the capital to invest in such risky investments that hold no promises of reaping the benefits (Cheah and Garvin, 2004). Instead, they adopt technological concepts which are centered on well proven technologies (generic in nature) or in close proximity to technologies that the companies are already using (Sexton, Barrett and Aouad, 2006).

Relative Technological Skills

Any contractor with unique or proprietary technological skills vis-à-vis other contractors is more likely to sustain its technology lead than a firm with imitable technologies, facilities and management technology (Porter, 1998, 2004).

Chapter 5

RESEARCH DESIGN AND METHODOLOGY

INTRODUCTION

This chapter first describes the research design and data collection method. Following this, the chapter explains the structure of the questionnaire and the targeted sample for the study. The chapter discusses how the collected data was analyzed. Descriptive statistics of the interviewees are presented and analyzed. The response rate of the research is assessed. The interviewees' designations and work experience in the construction industry are discussed. Lastly, the types of businesses and projects undertaken by the interviewees in the Singapore construction industry are briefly described.

RESEARCH DESIGN

In order to investigate and gain a deeper insight of the linkages between Porter's (1998, 2004) generic strategies and strategic practices in Singapore's construction industry to derive an understanding of competitive advantage for construction firms, a qualitative research approach was adopted. The research design was based on the questionnaire interview. The questionnaire included a cover page explaining the purpose of the interview and open ended questions, allowing the respondents to give unstructured answers with the opportunity to suggest a range of possible responses that may yet be unknown to the research team. Moreover, this approach helps to prevent bias in a list of possible responses. With less restriction in conveying their opinions, the respondents supplied fresh ideas and findings that may be difficult to express quantitatively. Respondents were guaranteed anonymity in the study.

The purpose of the questionnaire interview was to gather data on the strategic positions of contractors in Singapore, the impacts of these strategies and to examine whether these strategies still hold true in Porter's (1998, 2004) literature review on competitive strategy and competitive advantage. A copy of the questionnaire is given in Appendix 1.

DATA COLLECTION METHOD

As the questionnaire comprised open ended questions, the data collection method for this qualitative research adopted the face-to-face interview approach. In addition, this approach allowed clarifications of both questions and answers during the interview sessions. Following pilot testing, the questionnaire was both emailed and posted to the interviewees prior to the actual interviews. At the agreed time, interviews were conducted in their offices, which lasted between 60 minutes and 90 minutes. Several of the respondents also completed and returned the questionnaire by email. Follow-up email correspondences were undertaken when further clarifications were deemed necessary.

DATA COLLECTION INSTRUMENT

As shown in Appendix 1, the data collection instrument was a questionnaire which was specially designed for this study. The design started with the literature review relating to Michael Porter's works on competitive strategy and competitive advantage. The aim was to identity the various types of competitive advantage that contractors in Singapore may possess. Based on the literature review, and as noted earlier, the questionnaire was formulated based primarily on Porter's (1998, 2004) three generic strategies.

SAMPLING

The interviews were carried out from July to December 2007, targeting general contractors in the Grade A1 and Grade A2 categories in accordance with Singapore's Building and Construction Authority (BCA) registry of contractors.

However, the response rate was fairly low. The overall response rate of this research would be discussed later.

DATA ANALYSIS METHOD

Based on the literature review, three main types of competitive advantages were identified. The generic strategies are cost advantage (cost leadership), differentiation and focus. The interviewees were asked to categorize their firms in accordance with similarities in their respective strategies. The analysis was to determine the types of strategies adopted in Singapore's construction industry by different respondents. The impacts of these strategies were evaluated to determine their criticality and effectiveness.

The collected data in this qualitative research was analyzed using the deductive approach. This approach involved constant comparative analysis to generate knowledge about common pattern within the interviewees' experiential evidence in the Singapore construction industry. Thereafter, the responses were compared with Porter's (1998, 2004) generic business strategies to determine if the linkages were present (see research progression in Figure 1).

The analysis began by comparing the opinions made by the first two interviewees. The process continued with the comparison of data from the comments and inputs from each new interviewee, until all were compared with each other. The similarities or differences among the interviewees' responses were used to develop conceptualizations of the possible relations between various pieces of data.

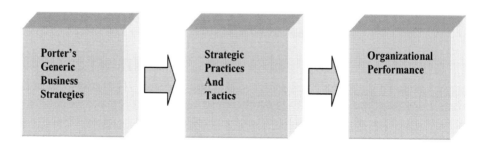

Figure 1. Research progression.

In this context, the data was collected mainly through face-to-face interviews with senior practitioners in the construction industry who have vast experience in managing construction projects in Singapore. The research method adopted for the study can be divided into four broad tasks:

Task 1 encompassed the literature review to source for background information. Porter's (1998, 2004) generic business strategies were then identified. The relevance of each of these generic strategies for construction firms was evaluated.

Task 2 encompassed the formulation and development of the questionnaire with respect to Porter's (1998, 2004) generic business strategies. The questionnaire was finalized following a pilot study with large construction firms in Singapore.

Task 3 encompassed the data collection phase that included consolidating the list of all large construction firms operating in Singapore. The questionnaire was sent to these construction firms through post and email. Face-to-face interviews were conducted with senior management personnel of these construction firms. Where further clarification was required, this was followed up with the interviewees by telephone and email.

Task 4 encompassed the data analysis stage where the responses provided by the interviewees were analyzed to determine if these correlate well with Porter's (1998, 2004) generic business strategies. The strategic positions adopted by construction firms were then established from the analysis. An in-depth case study of a large construction firm operating in Singapore was also conducted to elicit further information relating to and confirmation of an appropriate strategic management framework for large construction firms.

SAMPLE CHARACTERISTICS

In total, 57 requests for an interview were sent to the Grade A1 and Grade A2 general contractors in the Singapore construction industry. These were the two highest grades of registration for general contractors in Singapore. 25 respondents agreed to be interviewed, while two respondents returned the questionnaire via email. The overall response rate was 43.86 percent.

The poor response rate could be attributed to three main reasons. Firstly, some contractors were reluctant to share their business strategies, for fear of losing their strategic positions in spite of the assurance given by the research team on anonymity. Secondly, they explained that they were too overwhelmed with the amount of work during the then 2007 construction boom in Singapore and thus they declined to be interviewed. Lastly, several contractors were reluctant to be interviewed because the questionnaire involved a number of sensitive issues which they did not want to make their opinions known to the public. Again, this was in spite of the research team's assurance of anonymity and confidentiality.

Nevertheless, although the response rate is low, the data collected was still significant and meaningful as most interviewees were at senior management level in their respective companies and had vast amount of experience in the Singapore construction industry, as reflected in the discussions below. In addition, for those who participated in the study, they had all demonstrated great enthusiasm in the research and provided much precious information for the research team to garner a better understanding of the strategic framework and operations of the construction industry in Singapore.

PROFILE OF INTERVIEWEES

The construction firms were contacted to elicit their participation in the study. The persons contacted in each firm were those who are in the know or are authorized to provide the necessary information. Assurances were made to them that the purpose of the study was to analyze the strategic workings of the Singapore construction industry for academic purposes and that all information provided would· remain strictly confidential and the identities of the companies would not be revealed nor reflected in any way.

Table 1 shows that 40.74 percent of the interviewees were in senior management positions and 59.26 percent were in middle management positions. The senior management group comprised of managing directors, project directors and executive director. The middle management group comprised of business development manager, head of estimating and marketing, contract managers and project managers.

Table 1. Profile of interviewees

Profile	Frequency	Percent
Senior management	11	40.74
Middle management	16	59.26
Total	27	100.00

Table 2. Designations of interviewees

S/N	Interviewee code	Designation	Type of business	Generic strategy adopted
1	MC-7	General Manager	Public sector projects – wide range of projects	Cost advantage
2	MC-8	Deputy Manager	Public sector projects – wide range of projects	Cost advantage
3	MC-9	General Manager	Public sector projects – wide range of projects	Cost advantage
4	MC-10	Project Manager	Public sector projects – wide range of projects	Cost advantage
5	MC-11	Director	Public sector projects – wide range of projects	Cost advantage
6	MC-1	Executive Director	Public and private sector – private residential housing	Focus - Cost advantage
7	MC-13	Business Associate	Public and private sector – private residential housing	Focus - Cost advantage
8	MC-18	Executive Director	Public and private sector – infrastructure and sewerage projects	Focus - Cost advantage
9	MC-12	Business Development Associate	Public and private sector – infrastructure and residential projects.	Focus - Cost advantage
10	MC-14	Business Development Associate	Public sector projects – public housing projects, schools and commercial buildings	Focus - Cost advantage
11	MC-23	Deputy Manager	Public and private projects – private bungalow housing	Focus - Cost advantage
12	MC-24	Manager	Public sector projects – public housing projects, commercial buildings, upgrading and retrofitting	Focus - Cost advantage
13	MC-26	Project Manager	Public sector projects – public housing projects, schools and commercial buildings	Focus - Cost advantage
14	MC-6	Director	Private sector projects - commercial, mixed	Differentiation

			developments and luxurious residential housing	
15	MC-27	Managing Director	Private sector projects - commercial, mixed developments and luxurious residential housing	Differentiation
16	MC-3	Head of Marketing and Estimating	Private sector projects - commercial, retail and infrastructure	Focus - differentiation
17	MC-4	Deputy Manager	Private sector projects - commercial, retail and residential	Focus - differentiation
18	MC-5	Manager	Private sector projects - commercial, retail and residential	Focus - differentiation
19	MC-16	Project Director	Construction management type of procurement projects	Focus - differentiation
20	MC-17	General Manager	Private sector projects - commercial and retail	Focus - differentiation
21	MC-2	Project Director	Private sector projects - commercial, luxurious residential, retail and mixed development	Hybrid
22	MC-19	Senior Manager	Public and private sector projects	Hybrid
23	MC-20	General Director	Public and private sector projects	Hybrid
24	MC-22	Manager	Public and private sector projects	Hybrid
25	MC-15	Project Director	No specific type of projects	None
26	MC-21	Project Director	No specific type of projects	None
27	MC-25	Business Associate	No specific type of projects	None

The designations of the interviewees in their respective firms as shown in Table 2 indicated that they had insightful knowledge and years of work experience in the construction industry, thus ensuring the validity and accuracy of their responses.

The number of years of practice that the interviewees had in the construction industry ranged from five to twenty-five years:

1. 1 to 5 years – 8 percent
2. 6 to 10 years – 12 percent
3. 11 to 15 years – 20 percent
4. 16 to 20 years – 27 percent
5. 21 to 25 years – 33 percent

A majority (80 percent) of the interviewees had practiced more than 10 years in the construction industry and 60 percent of the interviewees had more than 15 years of experience. These results ensure a high level of credibility in the responses gathered from the interviews.

Table 2 shows that the interviewees were involved with building projects in different segments of the construction industry. The interviewees were involved in six types of projects: namely industrial factories, hotels, residential buildings, commercial buildings, infrastructural works and mixed development buildings.

This cross-section of building projects in the construction industry helped to ensure that the wide range of experience in the different types of projects was representative of the marketplace practices in Singapore.

Chapter 6

DIFFERENTIATION, FOCUS AND COST ADVANTAGE

INTRODUCTION

This chapter presents and discusses the interview findings with respect to the strategic framework and operations adopted by the larger Grade A1 and Grade A2 general contractors in the business of contracting in the Singapore construction industry. From the qualitative information collected, the research team seeks to look for patterns in the way companies create new tactics or re-create existing ones in relation to Porter's (1998, 2004) three generic business strategies.

Unless otherwise specified, the views presented below reflect those of the majority of the interviewees who participated in the study.

COST ADVANTAGE

The issue of cost is always a primarily concern among firms, in that they will go about reducing overall costs. However, the difference between all the interviewees relates to the extent of this concern. There are thirteen interviewees (MC-1, MC-7, MC-8, MC-9, MC-10, MC-11, MC-12, MC-13, MC-14, MC-18, MC-23, MC-24 and MC-26) who viewed cost as their most immediate concern than anyone else; five of the interviewees (MC-7, MC-8, MC-9, MC-10 and MC-11) belong in the same strategic group who competed purely on cost-based pricing (Best and de Valence, 1999) – full line, low manufacturing costs with moderate quality, but only two (MC-7 and MC-10) admitted that they have been consistently winning tenders by submitting the lowest bids. MC-7 explained that:

> "We offered the lowest price because we paid attention to things that have the greatest impact to us and this does not mean only raw materials such as concrete, formwork, reinforcement bars and labor. Also, we procured workers directly from China without a middleman."

Although MC-7 has successfully prioritized the chief cost drivers by grouping them together to coordinate the strategy of the firm, the general manager pointed out that the procurement of workers from China has been a tremendous driver to cut down on costs (unique access to cheap channels of distribution). Hence, this seems to undermine what Porter (1998, 2004) has advocated earlier. MC-7 has consistently enjoyed this low cost position especially through the hiring of low cost workers and did not find that the position of the firm is being imitated and eroded. This might probably illustrate that the construction industry in Singapore is still reliant to a large extent on labor intensive operations.

MC-7 continued to say that:

> "Many people think that we cheat in our pricing, that is, we will certainly make losses now then try to claim later. If this is correct, then how can our company survive from the financial crisis until now?"

This appears to underscore what Porter (1998, 2004) has been advocating relating to the importance of examining the entire value chain, instead of focusing only on items that have a huge percentage and/or impact on the budget such as those relating to raw materials such as concrete, formwork, reinforcement bars and labor. Therefore by breaking away from the conventional wisdom, they are still able to achieve a reasonable margin despite being the lowest bidder. This also appears to show that there are some "unique and unknown" commercial secrets that their rivals are unaware of. Such evidence differ from those presented by Ashworth and Skitmore (1983) who recognized that 80 percent of the entire construction costs are found in 20 percent of the items in the bill of quantities. In addition, such responses also contradict the findings presented by Lo, Lin and Yan (2007) who observed that firms submit suicidal bids at the risk of making losses. For that reason, these five main contractors recognized and managed to achieve cost effective and synergistic effects by exploring the interrelations and linkages in the entire value chain, in comparison to just 20 percent of items in the bills of quantities so as to achieve the lowest possible cost. This is echoed by MC-10 when his company also prioritized by using some form of information technology to control material handling, schedule deliveries and manage inventory. As MC-10 explained:

> "We tried to make money by compressing our activities together and time is money; otherwise all our efforts will go down the drain if we have to pay the time-imposed penalty or liquidated damages."

While MC-7 and MC-10 gained cost advantage by controlling the cost drivers in the value chain, MC-8 and MC-9 introduced radical and drastic measures by reconfiguring their value chain which agreed with Porter's (1998, 2004) proposition wherein firms can fundamentally restructure their costs than to be comfortable with incremental improvements. MC-8 explained that:

> "We have no choice but to change the way we work, otherwise we will be eaten alive by the dogs out there and these changes do not come automatically. After the financial crisis, a comprehensive review was undertaken to chart the company's mid and long term direction. One of the key strategies was to re-engineer our management expertise. This was seen as a fundamental leverage point to ensure our long term competitiveness."

MC-9 felt that in the age of globalization where the rules of competition have changed, it is nearly impossible for them to keep up with the pace if they are to still carry on about their old ways of doing business. MC-9 cautioned that:

> "There are so many hidden costs in projects that just adding a preferred margin to the costs can only happen during my grandfather's time. Now, we need to make more room to help us to be competitive".

Coincidentally, both MC-8 and MC-9 allowed for vertical integration by focusing on their manufacturing businesses of precast and pre-stressed patented components, prefabricated architectural metal components, increased ownership of equipment and modular formwork systems. MC-10 allocated for deeper integration where the firm developed its in-house expertise in building systems such as sanitary and electrical services; in so doing, the firm has created more linkages within its value chain. Such behavior displayed by these firms accord well with the observation presented by Raftery et al (1998) where the trend for increasing vertical integration in the packaging of construction projects was noticed in Asia. In this context, in-house systems are predominantly crucial for these firms where they are able to support greater competitive pricing, thereby by-passing the suppliers and/or subcontractor. In this manner, these firms can avoid having to benchmark their own profit margins above those set by others. As a result, the above elements have facilitated these firms greatly to work on a different production process as well as reducing cost in the form of gaining the appropriate scales of economies through market expansion and product lines extensions.

Apart from the above observations, only one contractor MC-9 stressed the criticality of both the tangibles and intangibles, through the importance of learning by gathering business excellence and practices regionally and globally, to serve as a guiding framework to improve the competitive standing of the firm which is similar to what Knuf (2000) has recommended earlier in "learning by doing".

It is observed that while the five construction firms provided the most competitive prices in the industry, this is not to say that the quality of their projects is compromised. Controlling costs and managing overheads to keep operations lean and efficient are the two foremost principles required from a cost-advantaged contractor and this strategy fits closely with Porter's (1998, 2004) cost advantage archetype. Moreover, it is evident that other than being efficient, the five firms reduced costs through their value chains and linkages. However, MC-11 felt otherwise. The director placed exclusive focus on primary activities in the construction sites where the costs of all inputs and tight overhead costs must be kept to the minimum, for example by controlling the number of employees working on site. To put it simply, it only remains necessary for the firm to keep a level of close control in the project phase to what was being allowed and contracted for during the tender stage. MC-11 felt that controlling these two major cost drivers are "more than enough"; otherwise "it would be a waste of resources". MC-11 also highlighted that:

> "Our company's financial strength, that is zero borrowing, and support from our banks are also our competitive advantage."

Therefore, what can be seen here is that MC-11's cost reduction policy concentrated on just bulky activities, but other activities that may possibly affect costs seem to have escaped the attention of management of the firm altogether, such as linkages among other major and minor activities and indirect activities, i.e. maintenance and inspection. Such an observation is in stark contrast to what Porter (1998, 2004) has earlier supported in the study of linkages among activities in the value chain. In addition, MC-11 opined that without borrowing from the banks, the firm can cut back on interests accrued on borrowed loans, thereby providing a lower tender price. Unfortunately, little did MC-11 know that all the other interviewees have also regarded their strong financial backing as a source of their cost advantage.

While the five interviewees acknowledged the criticality of their inward operations, there is another aspect that four interviewees (except MC-11) unanimously shared in helping them achieve their cost advantage position and that relates to the role of the subcontractors. As MC-10 explained:

> "No matter how good we are on our own, if we cannot control the subcontractors to work together with us, then it's futile. We want them to be successful every time they work with us; this is the way to retain them. We don't want to waste time working with and understanding our subcontractors every time we have a new project. "

MC-7 also highlighted that if the project is profitable to the other party, it will reduce the risks of delays. Unlike the main contractors, many subcontractors frequently work on multiple projects concurrently; thus they will allocate resources to those projects which in their opinion will bring them the maximum benefits (Sacks and Harel, 2006). Therefore, the four interviewees acknowledged that long term partnership with subcontractors is more desirable, instead on a project basis where sometimes the lowest price may not be the best offer as there might be more problems half way through the project. Hence, partnership is the most obvious choice in gaining the cost advantage, with both parties effectively sharing the mutual benefits. This is the main contractor who has an interest in convincing the subcontractors that they are in good hands; in return the subcontractors are able to give a more competitive rate, reducing the contingency portion for overheads (for supporting plant, equipment and facilities) that can be reliably provided for by the main contractor) as well as facilitating smooth project implementation. Hence, the subcontractors play an active role in contributing to the value chains of the main contractors through better integration of the linkages in the value chain. This accords well with the findings presented by Rahman and Kumaraswarmy (2004) on achieving long term cost savings through partnerships between the main contractors and subcontractors. However, this differs from the observations made by Allen and Helms (2006) who found that the cost advantage has only one significant strategy, which is to minimize distribution costs.

Apart from partnering with the subcontractors, MC-7 also described the importance of managing subcontractors in that:

> "We cannot push them too hard or be too lenient. During the good economic times now, if we push them too hard they will leave. Then during the bad times, if we push them too hard, they will also leave."

In MC-7's opinion, managing subcontractors by the main contractor is a complex matter. Pressurizing the subcontractors too much will cause them to leave the job due to the abundance of jobs that can be found elsewhere during good times. On the other hand, if times are bad, driving the subcontractors up the wall will cause them to go into liquidation which will also result in slow progress for the entire project. Likewise, MC-9 mentioned that the task of managing the subcontractors is a delicate matter because some subcontractors respond to different tactics differently (translated in Chinese, zhi luan bu zhi ying which means soft tactics work better than arm-twisting tactics for the subcontractors). Hence, in other words, there is no one size fits all approach; main contracting firms need to know when and what is the appropriate approach and time to improve the productivity of the subcontractors and to maintain a cordial working relationship with them.

Since five main contractors belonged in the same strategic group, naturally all of them shared a common objective of becoming a cost leader. This will have the tendency to increase the likelihood of repeated outbreaks of hardnosed price cutting until a single lowest bid prevails. This is in accordance with what Porter (1998, 2004) observed, that despite price cutting, the low cost contractors are still able to achieve a healthy profit margin as this position protects them from the five forces where the least efficient competitors are not able to endure such competitive pressures.

In spite of the observations made by Porter (1998, 2004) who reported that there should only be a single cost leader in one industry, it is noted that there are at least two firms who are cost leaders even though they are not market share leaders. Acknowledging this fact, MC-7's successful cost position in the industry was acknowledged by MC-8, MC-9, MC-10 and MC-11, where all of them knew that MC-7 was the leader in so far as cost advantage is concerned. As reiterated by MC-11:

> "If MC-7 enters a bid, we will run away. No point fighting. Everyone knows that they are very cheap."

Despite this, it is highly unlikely for the others to abandon the strategies to allow room for only one cost leader. A possible explanation for this is that it is unattainable for any single firm to monopolize the entire cost-advantaged segment of the construction market. This is unlike the market for Fast Moving Consumer Goods (FMCG) where it is usually a straightforward buy-sell relationship (Gann and Salter, 2000). Construction projects by nature often demand huge amounts of resources and attention that it is not possible for one firm to take up all the available projects, even if it wants to.

Owing to the uniqueness of construction projects, each contracting firm interlocks its activities together, where how one activity's cost is lowered because of the way other activities are performed to cater to the requirements of the client in the project, therefore making it difficult for others to imitate. This is because one cost-saving activity or linkage may work for one project but not necessarily for all the other projects. Thus, the main contractors are able to achieve cost advantage albeit in their own individual ways.

COST ADVANTAGE: FOCUS

The construction market in Singapore is too small for all the large contractors to compete for all the projects at the same time; while some competed broadly, others have chosen to dedicate their efforts to only one or a few segments in the industry.

Client-Focused

Out of eight contractors who subscribed to the cost advantage-focus strategy, there are four firms (MC-14, MC- 23, MC-24 and MC-26) who focused on price-sensitive buyers dealing with public sector projects, such as institutional facilities, Housing and Development Board's (HDB) apartments, upgrading and retrofitting works, and state-owned commercial buildings. MC-23 undertakes both private and public sector building works. In this context, public sector building projects abide by strict fiduciary provisions, unlike private sector clients where there is more leeway for exercising flexibility. This is due to the huge amount of financial resources which have to be stretched among multiple public building projects across the country. MC-14 agreed with this proposition and added that:

> "It is very hard to profit outside the contract in variations. Most specifications are very standard, just construct as you are told as they have tight budget, the client is very smart nowadays, gone were the days when you wish to make a windfall by variations."

For this reason, the main contractors will have generally know more or less how much they will be pocketing at the end of the project, given the client intelligence and expertise through repeated purchasing where they learnt to be very guarded against construction firms who have frivolously claimed on the grounds of variations.

Thus, the focus strategy appears to be somewhat different from the pure cost leadership strategy. While improving operational efficiency is important, there are other critical success factors such as quality and client service issues to address in the target segment. Firstly, in the opinion of all the interviewees, quality is important to ensuring low costs. In other words, they need to control the workmanship on site to make sure there is zero or minimum abortive work. This tendency is in line with what Allen and Helms (2006) have proposed. In this context, MC-24 opined that:

> "You need to have the right people with the right skills to work for you so that you get it done right the first time, which eliminates rework and scrap costs. Getting right the first time definitely reduce the costs wasted on materials."

MC-26 felt that his firm has improved its cost position by ensuring that the quality standards of the projects are fulfilled through conformance with specifications but did not exceed the clients' requirements. This is usually the case in public sector building projects where it is mandatory for the contractors to submit a conforming base tender before the awarding authorities would consider any other alternative tenders. This is because the authorities do not want to compare the prices between contractors on an equal footing. Hence, construction firms submit their proposed alternative tenders if they wish to deviate from the conforming base tender in an attempt to offer a lower bid price. However, such instances are not very common and MC-26 further mentioned that:

> "There is no need to provide fine quality buildings for our clients; they know how much they are paying us so in return they don't expect much from us, just as long as we build accordingly."

The term "quality" as defined here is by no means different from those of other firms, particularly those in the differentiation category. Low cost firms use moderate quality to reduce the direct capital costs for their buyers, while the differentiating firms offer high priced quality materials which can help their clients to reduce long term (indirect) servicing costs. Regardless of the quality of materials, it is more significant for the cost-advantaged firms to understand and identify the buyer's value such as the strict conformance to material quality and specifications in order to be an above-average performer.

Taking into account the above, extensive training and supervision of personnel working on site will not only serve to meet the customer's needs but also streamline processes to provide for cost efficiency. It is observed that MC-24 paid more attention to the staff – human resource management - as compared to the rest of the main contractors interviewed. The manager commented that:

> "We have gone the extra mile to provide for our workers. The company ensured the relevant competence of each worker through training and workshops and provided flexible work schemes to improve the productivity of our employees. On top of that, the company also organized monthly activities for company bonding."

Other than workshops and training to improve the productivity of the workers, MC-24 also introduced a flexible wage structure that not only increase productivity but also at the same time, reduce the firm's overheads. The firm realized that working on Saturdays is not productive, where a majority of the workers are reluctant to work on weekends and are willing to take a pay cut for the off-days. In response, the firm offered hourly paid wages for those workers who are willing to work on Saturdays. As expected, they experienced a drop in the number of people who return to work on Saturdays, yet productivity was not sacrificed.

From this episode, one can empathize why the company has conscientiously taken efforts to understand the needs of its employees. This provides a simple reason for the employees to be satisfied enough to stay with the company. As a result, it has also ensured a low turnover rate among the employees, hence helping to guarantee the quality of work completed through synergistic learning from one another. MC-24 affirmed that this is working well in that 85 percent of the workforce has been with the company for almost ten years.

The nature of the segment that these four contractors chose suggests that there is no need for them to increase the buyer's value or the buyer's performance through the exploitation of the buyer purchase criteria, particularly the signaling criteria as opposed to what Porter (1998, 2004) has recommended. As explained by MC-16 and MC-23, this is partly because in public sector projects, the client has, in almost all cases, the obligation to choose the lowest tender in order to be accountable to the paying public. Similarly, MC-14 commented that:

> "What matters to the government is the tender price; it does not really matter to them who you are, as long as you have experience. Everyone in the industry has experience!"

Thereafter, the above firms concentrated in their inward operations conscientiously, striving to lower their costs as much as possible without having to sacrifice their profit margins. However, Porter (1998, 2004) pointed out that there might be a danger in the future where firms may lack the ability to provide a "required product" because of the sole attention placed on costs.

One point worth noting in this client-focus strategy is that MC-23 has diversified into private housing projects, assuming the role of the main contractor as well as the developer, in order to narrow the gap between the interlocking roles of developer and contractor and hence, allowing more room for integration and better control of quality and workmanship standards. Nevertheless, the deputy manager cautioned that:

> "We should not try to compete with the big boys head-to-head in private housing. Our company has a niche in the cost advantage segment; we have customized ourselves to the specific segments. Therefore we will keep our private development as affordable as possible to target the public housing-up-grader market."

On the other hand, MC-14 thought that main contractors undertaking the role of developer is not advisable. He objected by noting that:

> "We become greedy and think about short term profits; I think construction companies should be more down-to-earth in sustaining their core expertise so that we all can become leaders in our respective areas".

The business development associate elaborated that construction firms should continually strive to improve their existing performance, as many firms are still not fundamentally strong enough. Hence, they should not venture into unchartered territories like property development. This was the advice given by MC-14 during the climate when there was en bloc sale frenzy among the property developers in Singapore.

Product-Focused

Apart from adopting the buyer-based focus strategy, the remaining four firms (MC-1, MC-12, MC-13 and MC-18) engaged in product-based focus in both private and public sector projects by staying in one area of core expertise; for example, either in infrastructure works, tunneling, sewage works or private residential projects. Construction firms have gained strong advantages through focus by using a target-centric value chain as compared to its broad-line competitors. MC-1 explained that strong benefits are being reaped because the:

> "Restructuring exercise is to improve the company's competitiveness in order to provide a comprehensive construction expertise to end-customers by eliminating any redundant activities."

Similarly with all the interviewees, everyone has taken a thorough examination of their value chains to diagnose and then to decide which activities are redundant and costly. This is in line with Porter's (1998, 2004) proposition, where firms should place importance on the value chain and the impact of its cost analysis on the company's costs.

Given the features of the large scale building projects as mentioned earlier, the interviewees were able to achieve economies of scale more efficiently. In addition, MC-12, MC-13 and MC-18 also felt that being a niche in a particular segment has helped them to direct all their attention to strengthen and sustain their existing competitive position, by heightening and deepening their existing barriers. MC-18 mentioned that his firm has undergone some changes to sharpen its business focus. His firm initially dabbled in businesses that included building materials, leisure, hospitality, construction and property development. His management decided to narrow this down to just solely on construction in order to be more efficient, thus committing most of the firm's resources to strengthen its foothold in this segment. In addition, MC-13 pointed out that:

> "Our competitive edge lies in our ability to keep costs low while providing innovative construction and developing concepts simultaneously."

Unlike the other three interviewees, MC-1 is a newcomer in this segment who has overhauled the entire value chain of the firm to specialize in smaller and mid-range residential projects, such as terrace houses and bungalows. This is because the management team decided to shift the firm to a more favorable strategic group in view of the intense competition in its previous strategic group. In addition, despite the fact that these projects are smaller in size, the company is able to accomplish as much yield as the larger projects without the need to bear significantly larger amount of risks. Such behavior has been explained by Porter (1998, 2006), where "specialist firms" are able to cushion themselves from industry rivalry. MC-1 ruled out involvement with long term projects or those that require large amount of resources. This is to minimize the firm's exposure to externalities which they may not be able to control. For this reason, MC-1 also explained that the smaller projects undertaken by his firm have insulated his firm from the effects of the recent sand ban imposed suddenly by the Indonesian government because the impacts were spread thinly among all the smaller projects. Consequently, the impact of the sand ban on MC-1 was very minimal.

Furthermore, MC-1 considered his firm to be in a more advantageous position as compared to its broadly targeted competitors, in terms of providing value added services. The firm provides luxurious housing at a more affordable price and value added services to enhance the value of its products, by having its own team of interior designers who can cater to the demands of the clients. Similar to what was described above, the executive director of the company highlighted that:

> "We conduct budgetary meetings with our quantity surveyors and accountants to make sure the credit and debit items are synchronized. We don't support front loading, even if our clients trust us and give us more money upfront, we will also refuse."

As can be seen from the above, focus strategies involving several segments rest on the presence of strong interrelationships; consequently, each contractor has built a focus strategy based on different interrelationships and different competitive advantages.

DIFFERENTIATION STRATEGY

Differentiation is one of Porter's (1998, 2004) key business strategies where firms focus on providing a unique product or service; this point was also reiterated by Hlavacka et al (2001). Both interviewees, MC-6 and MC-27, who are broad differentiators agreed with this statement in unison. What is worth noting is that these two firms are among the largest firms in the Singapore construction industry in terms of their capacities and resources. Approaches to differentiation can take place virtually in any activity. Hence, this is especially pertinent to these two firms (belonging in strategic groups A, B or C described earlier) who are competing against the entire construction industry whereby they will want to fully maximize the activities in the value chain from the primary to the indirect activities, from inbound logistics to service and so on. This preference was explained by MC-27 who noted that:

> "We are in a situation where we deemed that it is necessary to have brand image, technology, unique features, customer services and many others. For that

reason, we have the state-of-the-art technology to facilitate our group's operations in project planning, designing, construction, facilities management, maintenance, renovation and engineering in all sectors of the industry, all just to cater to different and complex needs of our customer."

The opinions of the interviewees demonstrate that their differentiation strategy should not stem from one activity in the value chain. Instead, if firms wish to accentuate the distinctiveness of the product, it will be more adept for them to examine the entire value chain, and marketing their cutting edge and proprietary technology to promote the high level of integration among activities.

In addition, both firms (MC-6 and MC-27) have many activities to support the complex, multi-tiered interactions as well as their exclusive technological expertise. Their differentiation strategies are therefore extremely difficult to replicate and could be possible permanent mobility barriers in the Singapore construction industry. This could mean that they may be involved in a tender where competition is very low. Their sustainability in differentiation thus fall in line with Porter's (1998, 2004) findings, where such companies continuously diminish their vulnerability to potential rivals with such strong drivers of uniqueness. In addition, this is also in line with the findings presented by Miller (1992) and Hambrick (1983) who suggested that differentiating firms are seen to provide two unique qualities which are proprietary technology and quality.

Another probable explanation could be that construction firms based in Singapore, with the exception of only a handful of firms, still lack the momentum to embrace the application of technology in their operations. Therefore, the use of highly advanced technology in all levels of construction i.e. from planning to the maintenance stage has certainly set these two firms apart from the rest of their rivals. Because of their commitments to such sophisticated (read expensive) technologies, it is next to impossible for these two firms to compete simultaneously in the low cost segment; with both interviewees citing that "it was not only uneconomical but also far too risky."

At a glance, these two firms seem to be identical in their pursuit of differentiation; however this is not the case, as both firms have employed different routes to differentiation. This strategy coincides with Porter's (1998, 2004) observations, which illustrate many ways to differentiating. Both interviewees not only have a pristine perception about their own position but also with respect to each other strategic position as well, wherein MC-6 commented that:

"Each company's policy and motto are very different. MC-27 offers the full package to their client – a set of comprehensive services. We operate from 'farm-to-fork', giving our clients the full assurance of our construction capabilities."

It can be seen from here that MC-6 prided his firm on integrating and coordinating activities, starting from planning the construction process involving equipment manufacturers, designers and engineers, all working towards achieving the project's needs and objectives. For example, MC-6 has managed to achieve dramatic reductions in defect rates by modifying every activity that influenced defects instead of relying on a single value activity - inspection. Similarly, its investments in indirect activities such as maintenance have improved the performance of its direct activities, by lowering the risk of product failure during the actual construction phase of the building. Consequently, this lowered the buyer's cost.

In the same way, MC-27's opinions indicated that his firm is the premier leader in Life Cycle Value (LCV), offering optimum solutions at every stage of the project life cycle and serving as the clients' life partner through facilities management. The opinion of MC-6 was indeed focused on the outstanding workmanship arising from the firm's Quality Assurance (QA)/Quality Control (QC) procedures, which helped the firm to accomplish an almost "zero defects" situation.

It is not therefore surprising to know that rivals from different strategic groups know of their superior differentiating abilities, causing MC-1 to recognize that:

"My company can never be like MC-6 and MC-27; they are too advanced in their technologies and work techniques. The amount of money that they pumped into their investments and research, I think it is equivalent to our annual turnover."

Notwithstanding the afore-mentioned, the two firms possess differentiating elements in their own rights but this alone is not going to be effective if the buyer did not value it. In order to be successful, their strategic positions must be understood and disseminated to the clients so that the latter will be willing to pay a premium price for their services. Both interviewees mentioned that the clients they served belong to a group of sophisticated or knowledgeable consumer, who are interested in the uniqueness of a product; thus their willingness to pay a price that is value for money. Furthermore, both directors clarified that a majority of their projects are not always secured through competitive bidding. MC-27 explained that:

"Many a times, we were invited on a negotiated contract basis with perhaps just one or two other companies. It is not rare that we are awarded the project even if we are not the lowest bidder."

Likewise, MC-6 pointed out that:

"In many instances, even though we were not the lowest, our clients often asked us if we could match up with the lowest tender or offer some other form of discounts."

Their experiences coincide with Porter's (1998, 2004) findings; that differentiation is undoubtedly costly as the firms have to sustain costs to be unique in a way that their clients value their services rendered to them. Each firm justifies a premium price, by reducing the buyer's cost through innovative technological leadership to deliver high quality buildings (MC-6) or raising the buyer's building performance in the total life cycle together with the use of sophisticated technological tools to better satisfy needs (MC-27). Therefore, both firms have preferred clients which lead to higher profit margins for them and high barriers to entry for other industry incumbents. This seems to go hand in hand with the findings presented by Allen and Helms (2006) where "innovation in technology and innovation methods" is the prime source of providing the best value through technology, which in turn can attract new clients as well as retain existing clients.

On the whole, the power of the buyer can be seen here as significant. Firms fulfill the needs of the clients through creating new value and delivering even higher added value. By means of customizing their procedures and operations, they are able to reap above-average returns from the premium price tag. Furthermore, the dedication between these two companies to serve their clients is indisputable, with MC-6 saying that:

"The company's goal was not to maximize profit at any costs. When customers are happy, our success is assured and profits will follow."

As can be seen from the above, both firms have no problems in providing state-of-the-art technologies. However, the promotion of their technologies to their clients remain a challenging task, where MC-27 pointed out that no matter how price insensitive their clients are, it would be futile if their clients do not perceive the value that they provide. This is especially so in the Singapore construction industry where fierce price competition prevails. Therefore, these two firms have to overcome the invisible barrier by showcasing their past projects and conducting realistic feasibility studies in educating their clients to appreciate the value added services offered to them.

This is a stark contrast to rivals in the cost advantage strategic groups, where there is an inward emphasis in its value chain, to minimize costs and the need to secure more projects to generate higher revenues. Here, differentiation is not about capturing market share; instead firms are generally more concerned about their capabilities to command a premium price to cover the technologies adopted and the high overheads. Moreover, with differentiation strategies, there is no need to raise revenues through multiple projects. The completion of a project provides a fine testimony of the firm's ability to deliver, resulting in almost invariably repeat orders from the same client. This is found to be consistent with the findings presented by Allen and Helm's (2006) as well as Mahmoud-Jouini (2000) where the actual product is the most effective form of marketing. This is also why the construction industry in general does not conduct any mass marketing strategies such as promotion and advertising because the successful completion of the project itself constitutes the most important form of advertising for the stakeholders involved.

This strategy has several interesting facets with MC-6 and MC-27 who competed through quality over price (Hambrick, 1983). Even though it appears evidently that they have sufficient cumulative experience that could allow them to be cost leaders, yet they opted for higher profit margins by competing on the premises of services and good image of the firm. This is evident in their discerning nature when it comes to the selection of projects. In this context, they will certainly not take part in tenders where there are more than four bidders because this will only undermine their differentiation strategies as well as their inability to engage in extremely competitive bidding.

DIFFERENTIATION: FOCUS

The differentiation – product focus factor again reiterated a unique product but this time to a smaller specialty niche. Firstly, through Porter's (2004) definition, the differentiation – product focus targets a specific market and with each providing a specialty product. With this in mind, the interviewees comprising of MC-3, MC-4, MC-5, MC-16 and MC-17 have the same common group of private sector clients. It is interesting to note that none of them have served the public sector clients. With respect to this, MC-3 highlighted that:

"It was not profitable enough to work with the public sector and to put it bluntly, our efforts were not recognized."

The response from MC-3 was supported by MC-14 who noted how the government awards projects to construction firms. Similarly, both MC-6 and MC-27 commented that differentiation on its own is accompanied by a hefty price. Competing for government sector projects is not an economical option since the method of operations and strategies of both low cost and differentiation are incompatible. Public sector jobs seem to offer the best merits to companies in the cost advantage group, which caused MC-4 to opine that:

"Private developers are less price sensitive and they can just pass the costs of construction to buyers of those properties; just divide the costs to the hundreds of occupants – it is peanuts."

The opinion of MC-4 demonstrates the importance of choosing the right selection of buyers (buyers with higher purchase power), so that a majority of the high costs of differentiation can be borne by occupants of the facilities. This is in line with Porter's (1998, 2004) proposition, where MC-5 also felt that the private sector can help his company to grow and possibly export its services overseas. MC-16 explained that it is less restraining to work for private sector clients, "more room to maneuver" in the absence of the strict conformance to specifications. This is because of the use of other types of procurement systems such as design-and-build and management contracting instead of the traditional procurement mode based on bills of quantities. The second part of the statement appears to refute Porter's (1998, 2004) observation. Even if construction cost is a significant cost in the overall budget, buyers are still rather price-insensitive. However, price is a major factor that deters differentiating companies from competing in the public sector. In this context, MC-17 clarified that:

"The homogeneity of these projects leaves us out in the running for such projects. It is more suitable for companies which are efficient and cheap than to be unique and expensive."

Judging by the various responses above, it seems that all the interviewees have been selective over what the types of projects and who their clients are. They are generally concerned with how they can fully exploit their differentiating advantage as well as the growth potential of a buyer. In Porter's (1998, 2004) opinion, a good buyer is not one that necessarily pays well. Instead, to a large extent, other spin-offs can generate positive strategic implications, such as improving the firm's existing competitiveness or to eventually export its expertise overseas. In this connection, MC-17 commented that:

"There is no need to take up so many projects. We have to conduct a thorough project analysis to measure the risks and how the project can benefit. A well constructed project speaks for itself."

The above comment implies that in comparison to the overall differentiator, the differentiation focuser identifies segments and buyers with unique and special needs, which they can then better meet. On the other hand, the former bases its strategy on widely valued attributes.

Focus is also based on adopting a narrow competitive scope such that all the interviewees have carved out their niches in certain procurement systems or in different sectors of the Singapore construction industry. Some firms enjoy sole exclusivity in the niche area, while others have to share the pie among one another. Regardless of which segment the firms are located, different sources of differentiation have surfaced.

All interviewees, except MC-4, felt that it is more important for their companies to be nimble and flexible in their operations and strategies in order to cater to the demands of their clients especially so in supporting some of their clients' other ad-hoc projects. This is reflected in the findings presented by Allen and Helm (2006), where providing outstanding customer service is the next most critical element after quality control for companies in the differentiation - focus category. MC-3 underscored such importance by stating that:

"Being flexible creates a faster response time to the clients. We need to be swift in our decision making. Any time wasted would reflect how inefficient the company is to satisfying our clients. We cannot afford this."

This approach is in contrast to the broad-differentiation strategy, where "innovation in technology and construction methodology" is an influential determinant.

Being different will hardly suffice to be called a differentiator. Thus, the interviewees were asked why they thought they belonged to this differentiation – focus category. MC-3 noted that his firm's operations have been restructured, creating leaner supply chain management from the procurement and handling of inputs, responsiveness to changes and defects, excellent relationships with clients and a pool of regular suppliers of high quality products. MC-3 added that all of these were meticulously managed and controlled without out-sourcing to third parties. MC-5 aligned the position of his firm with stringent risk management and expertise in facilities management through the adaptation of its diagnostic protocol and comprehensive service packages. Interestingly, MC-16 is the sole company in the industry at the current moment that provides a full range of construction management services. In other words, MC-16 is a "non-contractor" who handles the procurement of materials from raw materials to furniture and fittings as well as overseeing and coordinating the construction works on site to ensure smooth project delivery. Hence, this eliminates the need for the middle man through procuring directly on behalf of its clients. This in turn results in maximizing its bargaining power and thereby differentiates itself from others.

Lastly, the firm which MC-17 belongs to has in-house multi-disciplinary design divisions coupled with an architectural and engineering subsidiary. With different divisions under the firm, this presents a better integration of the fragmented process where parties used to work in isolation. Such integration will enhance project performance and deliverables and minimize discrepancies between the designs of different parties. For instance, the structural design is customized in-house to improve the constructability of the project by taking into account of the architectural aspects of the same project.

Based on the experiences of the interviewees described above, what each of them have provided are related to sources of differentiation, such that the "focusers" manage to tailor their value chains to cater to the various "unusual" needs of the buyers in the focus segment. In the absence of stable prices and market shares in an industry, this pathway appears to be a realistic strategy to consider in both broad and focus differentiation.

On the other hand, with MC-4 placing his firm in the focus-differentiation category, the deputy manager said that:

> "We offer quality buildings to our clients. This is our competitive advantage."

In this context, it may be the case that MC-4 may have misunderstood Porter's (1998, 2004) definition of the term "differentiation", because MC-4 appeared to define it by means of quality where the firm viewed itself as a "Quality Builder". The firm appears to differentiate itself using quality, even though it is lacking in focus as it did not involve any significant differential value chain offered by its competitors. This scenario seems to align well with Porter's (2004:16) case study, where Porter (2004) referred to an unsuccessful soft drink firm (Royal Crown) competing on the basis of the differentiation focus strategy:

"In soft drinks, Royal Crown has focused on cola drinks, while Coca-Cola and Pepsi have broad product lines. Supplying only colas does not involve a significantly different value chain than supplying a broad line. Buyer needs is not much different for colas. Hence Royal Crown's strategy leads to no competitive advantage against its competitors, only disadvantage (Porter, 2004:16)."

If the above example is taken within the context of the construction industry, then MC-4 will be the equivalent of Royal Crown, who defined differentiation too narrowly and failed to differentiate the firm from other rivals in the same industry. This is not just a simple process of market segmentation; rather the value chain involved in producing the product consists of economic tradeoffs between cost and quality, production and other functional supports. Moreover, MC-4 was not able to provide further information on how the firm goes about producing the quality products as claimed. For the low emphasis placed in the differentiation issue, it can be ascertained that MC-4 did not seem to place much emphasis on the processes involved to get to the final product. Rather, MC-4 placed too narrow attention merely on the quality of the materials used. In this case, the position of MC-4 in the construction industry is different but not differentiated as the firm is already providing services that are widely available in the industry. In consequence, the "ordinary" position of MC-4 in the differentiating segment will be very much contested in view of the increasing competitive pressures ahead.

Most of the interviewees agreed that customer service is one vital element when it comes to competing in the niche segment. However, there is one common point that is shared between the broader and focus differentiators and that relates to the need for the buyers to recognize their core expertise. This was highlighted by MC-17 who had recently conducted a "customer service survey" which reported that:

"We had relatively low performance ratings given on 'being innovative' and possessing 'an ability to give adept design solutions', both being our core values."

MC-17 was surprised with the results as his firm has been providing such services to its clients consistently for several years which have often facilitated the construction process and sometimes helping the client to save costs. However, it is apparent that the results showed that being unique does not guarantee differentiation. One possible reason that could account for such dismal results could be that the firm has created value that is not well valued by its clients. This seems to suggest that they have been targeting the wrong group of clients. This is in line with Porter's (1998, 2004) findings, in that a successful differentiator must find ways to generate relevant value for the buyers. With this mind, the management staff of MC-17 decided to take immediate actions to better understand their clients, examine their implementation strategy and to promote the firm to benefit both the firm and the client. Otherwise, the firm may never be able to command the price that it actually deserved.

Overall, the strategies and tactics adopted by the interviewees towards broad and focus differentiation have indicated that it is possible for the construction industry to have more than one leader as compared to the cost leadership in the cost advantage segment. Although there is no empirical evidence to support that differentiation strategies are more profitable than cost leadership strategies, for two reasons, it can be suggested that differentiating firms appear to be more profitable. Firstly, with a differentiation strategy, the decisions of the clients do not just take into consideration of price alone. Instead, many other attributes are considered such as quality, technical capabilities, customer service and reputation of the firm that can be used to quantify buyers' perceived value which one would expect to match with the ability of the firm to deliver the final product as promised. Quite on the contrary, with a low cost strategy, the primary decisions of clients on projects are determined by price, such that prices are compared with the cost structure of the next competitor. Hence, this leaves the construction industry to be worse off from the standpoint of profitability. Secondly, investments in technology and renewal are likely to persist, especially for firms who are currently investing actively in technology. By doing so, they are hoping to stay ahead of exiting rivals and discouraging potential entrants, thus amounting to creating barriers to entry. Hence, it appears that greater margins could usually be achieved with differentiation by first overcoming the industry structure.

Chapter 7

HYBRID STRATEGIES

INTRODUCTION

The exclusivity of the three generic business strategies as proposed by Porter (1998, 2004), especially with respect to cost advantage and differentiation and how these strategies are mutually exclusive, was discussed earlier. These formed the initial thoughts about Porter's (1998, 2004) generic business strategies for individual assimilation and effective applications in the construction industry.

Notwithstanding the afore-mentioned observation, four interviewees (MC-2, MC-19, MC-20 and MC-22) in the field study have chosen a combination approach to applying these strategies. By combining the afore-mentioned generic strategies, it is argued that the hybrid strategy could well be equally successful for competition. Each strategy on its own has had a considerable amount of success. Anecdotal evidence provided by the four interviewees suggest that the two strategies are not necessarily compatible in isolation, thereby appearing to contest the validity of Porter's (1998, 2004) stance on the exclusivity of these competitive advantage strategies. MC-2 will be the focus of a case study to be presented later; for this reason, the firm shall not be included as part of the discussion in this section.

Although there could be many permutations on the different combinations of generic strategies, such as low cost-differentiation (focus), low cost (focus)-differentiation and many others, all the interviewees explained that their combination strategy is to enable them to compete simultaneously (broad scale) on low cost and differentiation. Within the context of the construction industry in Singapore, MC-22 recognized that while the recent importance of technological expertise and quality have played a significant role in influencing the outcome of its client's decisions, price is still nonetheless a major concern among clients. Therefore, it can be deduced that there is yet another class of buyers between low cost and differentiation. Hybrid strategies are said to be preferred when clients are concerned with the many aspects of a product, such as price, quality and features; in other words, buyers who want their project budget to achieve "value for money" and "affordable yet high quality" as noted by MC-20.

MC-20 added that using a hybrid strategy is more suitable for the local palette, as the Singapore construction industry in its earlier days (and there are still traces) generally placed an over-emphasis on the lowest price. As a result, many construction firms went bankrupt; in a large part this was a made-in-Singapore phenomenon. This perhaps highlights the fact that the choice of a hybrid strategy will not only help the firms but also the industry's structure by becoming a "good competitor", by steering away from the pressures of notorious price cutting. This outcome has created a paradox, by agreeing to Porter's (1998, 2004) statement to becoming a good competitor, yet this was accomplished through the adaptation of hybrid strategies rather than utilizing Porter's (1998, 2004) pure generic strategies.

In addition, on the subject of differentiation, MC-20 and MC-19 felt that the pie is more than sufficient for everyone in the industry, unlike some industries in which a single homogenous product is sold to all buyers. Thus, none of the interviewees have revealed any plans to expand overseas in the near future. MC-19 who remained unfazed by the numerous rivals that his firm faces in the construction market claimed that:

> "We are not selling an entirely homogenous product like chemicals or fertilizers. Quite the reverse, buildings are far from being homogenous. They contained many attributes and thus the promise of greater scope for differentiation and costs."

Because of the above perception, none of the interviewees thought that pursuing a pure strategy relative to their rivals will be more beneficial than hybrid strategies. Other than the uniqueness of the construction industry, all the interviewees felt that there is a mandatory need for construction firms to be more competitive in other dimensions, besides costs. Considering that competing on the low cost strategy alone is only effective towards price sensitive clients will create incessant price pressures in which enormous detrimental effects will inevitably harm the firms and the overall industry structure. Thus, this assertion seems to support Porter's (1998, 2004) views of advancing towards maintaining a stable industry structure without unnecessary rivalry.

The differentiating firms appear to be the ones who have been successful in avoiding competitive pricing in the construction industry. Unfortunately, the quest for such strategic position will be an uphill struggle for these firms as previous discussion above seemed to prove that these traits do not appear to characterize most construction firms here in Singapore. In the study presented below, a range of problems in relation to technology have been identified to characterize a majority of the construction firms in Singapore: lack of financial and technological resources, traditional methods used and low labor productivity. Despite clear indicators to show that there have been efforts to change, the fact remains that there is still a handful of firms who are still inherently disadvantaged in pursuing pure differentiation strategies, especially against the more established firms (MC-6 and MC-27). Such a predicament was reiterated by MC-20 who disclosed that his firm has initially accomplished a low cost position, but had since broken away from the pack and now compete head to head with other firms:

> "Low cost tender will make us back to square one with low profits and yet we are in no position to compete with pure differentiated firms. Being sandwiched, we can get the best of both worlds."

Hence, firms who are caught in the low cost predicament will see them revert back to their old ways, owing to the insurmountable task of becoming truly differentiated. Quite on the contrary to Porter's (1998, 2004) propositions, the use of a hybrid strategy provides a relief for firms who wish to break out of the vicious low cost cycle and move towards differentiation, by means of incremental small steps. To such a degree, the firms are able to compete concurrently both on the low cost and differentiated basis. However, one might ask, what exactly are the ingredients that promote the thriving hybrid strategies, especially in the context of the construction industry in Singapore?

There are two plausible explanations that could account for this phenomenon. Firstly, the construction industry in Singapore is fragmented in terms of structure and operations (Construction 21 Steering Committee, 1999). This suggests that there are too many segregated parties within the industry where it will be inherently difficult to categorize firms neatly into the generic strategies. Furthermore, the construction industry cannot be divided into two distinct sectors – quality (differentiation) and cost (low cost) as many other attributes reflect the fluctuating preferences of the buyers, such as technology, cost, quality, service and so on. Secondly, Porter (1998, 2004) appears to have overlooked the dynamism, complexity and other external factors, i.e. competitive behavior of rivals, resource availability, and time constraints, which make up the modern economic markets of today, especially in construction. Consequently, this is by far the more complex hurdle to resolve than to label firms into just the three generic strategies. In addition, given the nature of the construction industry, it is not possible for a single or a handful of firms to monopolize the entire business in the industry. Instead, what is found in the Singapore construction industry is a myriad of strategies adopted by firms, and that contrasted with what Porter (1998, 2004) had advocated earlier for two distinct types of firms.

Through such hybrid strategies, the firms can, on the one hand, attain a reasonable cost against their rivals who pursued cost advantage strategies. On the other hand, they can close the gap with pure differentiators and possibly derive additional benefits from their lower cost position. Hence, it appears beneficial to have more than a few dominant firms in the construction market which will be good for competition, albeit a different kind of competition from price. With this in mind, MC-19 shared that:

> "During the Asian financial crisis, I can say that we are better off than most people, we not only received repeated orders from clients but also were asked by other clients to take over uncompleted (abandoned) projects."

The senior manager went on to explain that during the 1997 Asian financial crisis, many clients found themselves sabotaged by contractors who abandoned their projects because of negative cash flow problems because the latter have submitted unrealistically low bids. In addition, many clients were not able to afford "branded" contractors. The use of the hybrid strategy therefore allowed his firm to capture more of the market share during such times and established a name for itself in technical excellence and for being financially healthy. This has since then given his firm an edge over its rivals.

Along this line of reasoning, the viability of the hybrid vis-à-vis pure strategies seems by far more convincing as an alternative for firms. This approach conforms to the findings presented by Hlavacka et al (2001), Helms, Clay and Peter (1997) as well as Johnson and Scholes (1999) where hybrid strategies were found to be equally viable or even better within an industry. However, this differs vastly from the findings presented by Porter (2004:18) who asserted that: "generic strategies become inconsistent and a firm must make a choice".

Contrary to the experience shared by MC-20, MC-6 disagreed that the benefits of optimizing a pure strategic choice cannot be gained if a firm wants a share in every segment of the industry. In other words, hybrid firms will lose focus in their core activities. In spite of these two conflicting views, it is evident that in the Singapore context, it is still feasible for firms to achieve above-average performance in either the pure or the hybrid generic strategies, judging by the success of firms competing in both segments.

All interviewees related the "Total Quality Management" (TQM) perspective as an ideal solution for construction firms to gain a competitive edge over their cost advantage rivals. The key reason is that through TQM, they are able to improve quality and cost savings through the use of Just-In-Time (JIT) control of materials delivered to site, sound purchasing practices and strict quality control, and subsequently, offering their clients a better product at competitive prices. To reiterate, Smith and Reece (1999) stressed that quality and cost strategies are by no means independent; on the contrary, they can be jointly supportive. MC-19 explained that TQM activities are effective means of developing, maintaining and improving construction and customer service related activities through their four essential principles – quality, costs, delivery and safety – and that:

> "We tried to provide a balance between quality and costs (affordable price) while meeting deadlines and safety requirements by providing integrated solutions to each creation."

This experience appeared to be similar to the results reported by Hill (1988) as well as Spanos, Zaralis and Lioukas (2004), which found that the notion of TQM had eroded the traditional belief that "quality is expensive". This similarity in findings could be due to the fact that hybrid firms in the Singapore construction industry generally make a choice by pumping in more capital to realize the interactions through the use of technology. Besides this, MC-22 adhered to a defined framework of TQM that incorporates technology to complement the firm's operations and procedures through from the stages of design and production to post-completion by:

1. Defining the customer's needs.
2. Translating them to tangible design specifications.
3. Faithful building by "Quality of Conformance".
4. After completion, implementing quality assurance activities through after-sales service.

Other than the TQM framework that the interviewees have in common, they also shared several responses that are similar to those of their competitors, where they asserted that it is imperative for them to be efficient by minimizing their production costs through exploring the many possibilities within the value chain. MC-20 gave one example on the procurement strategies in his firm which has a permanent relationship with several suppliers on raw materials and custom built fittings and furniture. The suppliers have customized one of their production lines to suit the needs of MC-20. As a result, the suppliers are able to respond swiftly, quality is assured and discounts are passed on to MC-20, with the suppliers reaping economies of scale. In this context, the practice appears to be aligned with Porter's (1998, 2004) observations where working with suppliers can exploit vertical linkages.

The interviewees' responses indicate their low cost advantages against their low cost rivals but the question remains whether their hybrid strategies have placed them in a position to compete simultaneously in the pure differentiation category, like what Spanos, Zaralis and Lioukas (2004) claimed on closing the gap on pure differentiating firms. In response, MC-20 explained that the ideal is to reach what MC-6 and MC-27 have achieved; they wanted to improve and to compete for the same customers. As MC-20 clarified:

> "There is no question about their abilities (pure differentiators) but are they able to compete on competitive prices like ours when their technologies are so expensive?"

Apart from the low cost rivals, all the interviewees appear to be confident in sustaining their presence in the construction industry in spite of the technological superiority of the pure differentiators. The reason is that the hybrid firms see the demand of buyers who seek quality at affordable prices that the pure differentiators are unable to provide or buyers who are unable to afford to pay for the services of the pure differentiators. This too explains that regardless of pure or hybrid strategies, firms can be equally successful if they are able to meet the specific needs of the construction industry and at the same time, sustaining their individual unique competitive advantages.

The hybrid firms also saw the importance of managing people (subcontractors) and teamwork on site, citing that "it's a human game" and as MC-22 explained:

> "It's all about human management, whether it's your own colleagues or with external parties, different personalities are bound to clash. We all need to learn how to work together on site. If everyone puts on a black face, then the project will not be able to carry on smoothly."

This suggests that cohesiveness among people, amidst all the technicalities in the construction industry, constitutes an influential factor towards the success of any building project.

Furthermore, MC-19 was also quick to add that despite with technology, the increasing complexity of construction activities had not been made easier. Instead it has become tougher as more personnel from the different disciplines are needed. In other words, human glitches are often the hardest to resolve and possibly the increasing complexity of building projects has ironically lead to the demise of modern technology.

In general, hybrid firms have demonstrated their abilities to deliver both costs and quality targets to their clients. Thus construction firms cannot underestimate and undermine the capacity of such strategy, for this might hold the key to a different landscape of competition for the construction industry in the near future.

STUCK IN THE MIDDLE

Three interviewees (MC-15, MC-21 and MC-25) did not categorize themselves into any of the above categories, as opposed to the rest of the interviewees who have one way or another identified themselves with specific types of strategies. In this context, the three firms placed a moderate emphasis on all generic strategic dimensions and have said to compete on the broad and focus segment areas. Hence, according to the definition offered by Miller and Dess (1993) of such strategic behavior, this would amount to a particular type of underdeveloped hybrid strategy, where firms lack a distinctive emphasis on any strategies. These firms are either at the losing end and picking up the "leftovers" or this could be the preferred alternative considering the difficulties for these firms to take up pure differentiation or cost advantage position to avoid cost pressures.

All three firms felt that it is more appropriate for them not to have specific strategies, fearing that this will inhibit their abilities to compete in different sectors. This is similar to how the interviewees felt earlier, where using a mixture of low cost and differentiation strategies will help them to be more competitive in both sectors. To support this argument, MC-25 said that:

"Construction is a hands-on business where you plan your strategy only after you have successfully been awarded the project."

Adding on, MC-21 further mentioned that site conditions and the various construction methods are never static or the same; instead they are always different in every project. Hence, he felt that the most appropriate strategy is to overcome the site conditions, plan accordingly to the characteristics of the project and not the other way round like what the rest of the interviewees have done. He emphasized further by noting that:

> "We can do any project. It all depends on risk management studies done on site and suitable construction methods to determine the profitability of the project."

The reason for such a strategy could be that these firms believe in the most practical approach to profitability by understanding the nature of the projects and then applying the suitable construction methods. In addition, it can also be inferred that the way these firms executed their strategies did not determine the particular segment that they have to compete in, unlike the rest of the interviewees, where policy choices may perhaps limit their market coverage. The behavior of this group of interviewees agreed with the findings presented by Low and Abdul Aziz (1993) where the strategies which the firms made may be indefinable and that the success is highly dependable on the requirements of the project. However, this differs with Porter's (1998, 2004) observations where it appears mandatory for firms to come to a decision between the generic strategies in order to gain a competitive advantage position. Further elaboration on Porter's (1998, 2004) findings suggests that the presence of such firms seems to reflect that the construction industry in Singapore is still not efficient enough to eliminate "unfocused" firms, which are still not exposed to the vagaries and real impact of competition.

MC-15 defended his position by pointing to Singapore's open market economy which has led to the low barriers to entry; hence, the project director opined that:

> "Every firm is free to come in and make a living, because of the lack of protectionism of the industry by the government."

Although MC-15 did not mention the lack of protectionism by the government in Singapore, he pointed out that given the level of economic freedom in Singapore he felt it is more appropriate for his firm not to be rigid. Instead the firm should seize every opportunity as it comes. This implies that barriers of entry into the market in Singapore is low and easy. Hence, in relation to Porter's (1998, 2004) analysis of the industry structure, profit margins are likely to fall in view of the ease of entry into the market. Given the likely influx of competitors into the market, both MC-21 and MC-25 felt that it will be ironical to have a fixed strategy when the competition is never stagnant; they agreed that speedy response is an important ingredient to success.

While all three firms are competent in their respective field of works, however, such internal focus on short term challenges might prevent them from recognizing their shortcomings because these firms are not guided by an overall strategic assessment to safeguard their long term interests. This may be perilous if they continue to concentrate only on short term interests, which may has widened the gap between themselves and the industry, creating the higher possibilities of letting the industry to return to the times of aggressive price wars. As mentioned above, partnerships present positive strategic implications where both parties share common long term interests. For this reason, MC-21 and MC-25 might lose out on the advantages of forging long term strategic partnerships.

The above observation is to be read in comparison with the inputs from the rest of the interviewees, who appear to take at least one distinctive strategic position. This observation did not seem to accord with the findings presented by Allen and Helms (2006), Porter (1998, 2004), Wright (1996) as well as Hambrick (1983), which found that strategies within firms are meant to be a guide for the firms. Without any strategy, firms can easily find themselves losing sight of the reasons for their success and thereby compromising the growth of the firm.

TECHNOLOGY

It is widely acknowledged that Singapore's construction industry pales in comparison with other technologically advanced sectors of the national economy such as those in the sciences, information technology and manufacturing. Hence, the construction industry in Singapore is perceived to be bordering on "low technology". However, one may ask what exactly defines technology? On this count, all the interviewees gave similar answers. These included terms like advance and expensive technology, innovation and new technology. According to Porter's (1998, 2004) definition of technology, this should be considered within the entire value chain, thus taking the view into a much broader consideration.

Technology and Value Chain

All interviewees have adopted different forms of technologies to varying degrees throughout the value chain, depending on the adoption of their respective strategic groups. The sections below examine how firms have used technologies to wield competitive advantage in their favor.

In the first category, interviewees (MC-4, MC-11, MC-12, MC-14, MC-23 and MC-25) have said to have invested in *enabling technologies* (Sexton, Barrett and Aouad, 2006). The technologies invested would fall under the vital type of technologies such as equipment (cranes, crawler, and excavators), information technology systems supporting the firms, infrastructure including office support and scheduling activities on construction sites and other forms of construction technology that have been tried and tested before.

In the second category, a majority of the interviewees (MC-1, MC-5, MC-7, MC-8, MC-9, MC-10, MC-13, MC-17, MC-18, MC-20, MC-21, MC-22, MC-24 and MC-26) have engaged in *enabling and critical technology* (Sexton, Barrett and Aouad, 2006), with investments ranging from self-manufactured pre-cast and fabricated technology, advanced communication technology via blackberry, computer aided design technology, procurement and logistical technology for reporting, scheduling and implementation, training workshops to equip employees with suitable technologies and last but not least, information technology such as the Virtual Private Network (VPN) and central intranet systems that pervade the entire value chain to facilitates linkages among activities.

In the third category, some of the interviewees (MC-2, MC-3, MC-6, MC-15, MC-16, MC-19 and MC-27) have made use of *critical technology* (Sexton, Barrett and Aouad, 2006) in the form of proprietary, innovative construction and engineering technology, establishing divisions within the company for R&D activities, various in-house specialist fields, advanced training workshops and advanced information technology systems to support the entire operations and procedures of the business.

Technology and Competitive Advantage

Technology and Cost Advantage

All interviewees in the first category of *enabling technology* belong to the low cost segment (MC-11, MC-12, MC-14 and MC-23), with the exception of MC-4 and MC-25. Their approach to technology is limited to commonly used technologies which are widely available to all competitors in the construction industry. For instance, the use of computer software such as MS Project and Primavera for scheduling purposes and to managing inventories closely, thus leading to process efficiency.

Secondly, the firms have focused on the careful management of their assets and equipment, making sure that capacity is maximized in order to reduce overall costs. This finding aligned well with the observations presented by Hambrick (1983) who considered this to be a realistic strategy. However, Porter (1998, 2004) warned that increasing complexity (for example, in the technological sense) will raise the costs of coordination that can easily result in diseconomies of scale. Despite the low levels of technology and having no consistent differential advantage, the firms are still able to create a clear competitive strategy and achieve average or above-average results.

Being in the low cost strategy segment coupled with only enabling technologies, will place these interviewees in a precarious situation, especially when the Singapore construction industry is moving towards the age of the knowledge-based economy and rapidly changing demands from buyers (Ofori, 2002). In response, the technology strategy of a firm can potentially be a vital factor in enhancing its overall competitive strategy. Even if the construction industry appears to accommodate this operating environment currently, nevertheless there remains a possibility for this category of firms to be left behind.

According to all the interviewees, it is not as clear-cut as it seems for them to consider the use of more technology in their construction projects. MC-11 lamented that the projects undertaken by his firm are usually secured on thin profit margins and that there is just not enough money to mete out for investments in other "extra technologies". He explained that the technologies which his firm used are:

> "The technologies that were just enough to keep the office running and as for construction wise, we import some machines that can be used to improve the productivity of our construction workers, like mechanized handheld equipment."

As a result, all four interviewees (MC-11, MC-12, MC-14 and MC-23) preferred to hold on to their assets – holding down investments in technology and preferring to take matters into their own hands through the expertise of their site staff. Moreover, MC-12 further justified that technology is helpless when it comes to problem solving; thus, this is where the project site staff comes in to apply damage control. According to the interviewees, it can be surmised that it is not possible for the Singapore construction industry to move away from being labor intensive to being capital intensive. This is because there will be an irreplaceable demand for labor, especially when the bulk of the construction activities involves assembly and installation of building components on site. This is also being exemplified in MC-23's response where he mentioned that his firm's additional equities are used to venture into private development of properties rather than in the investments of technologies. The firm's motive can be understood as undertaking of the role of the developer appears to be more lucrative where perceived benefits seem to be more tangible than the investments in technologies.

Another possible explanation could be that the predominant procurement system of design-bid-build in the low cost segment is in line with the observations made by Dulaimi et al (2002), where one of the more important requisites for technology and innovation draws from the type of procurement systems and where traditional design-bid-build places the contractors in a more passive role towards accepting and utilizing technology. Hence, in view of this, quality is defined to mean the conformance with specifications as mentioned earlier and where MC-11 described it as "no-frills" construction when he explained that:

> "What you see on the drawings are exactly what the clients get, nothing more, nothing less."

Along the same line of reasoning, the interviewees expressed their satisfaction in the way their businesses are being managed that they disagreed on how the use of technology can be useful to them in the near future, as more technology meant they will not be able to stick to their "no-frills" construction. In addition, two out of the four interviewees perceived that more technology also meant a reduction in their financial reserves. MC-23 explained that construction business is all about managing risks. Thus the control of cash flow is an extremely delicate task as any unforeseen events on the construction site will translate into negative profits for the firm. These could include risks such as inclement weather or unfavorable site conditions, inaccurate measurements in taking-off quantities, changes in the scope of work relating to the design of the building and the inadequate provision of manpower resources. Therefore the surplus in the financial reserves will be extremely useful to prepare them for such situations when the project risk allowance is insufficient. In this context, it appears that firms had mistakenly assumed that technological change is not targeted at cost-oriented firms but intended for enhancing differentiation. MC-4 added that:

> "Because of the extremely competitive arena, our contingency sums cannot be too high; otherwise it is as good as throwing the prospective project out of the window."

On the other hand, not all firms competing in the low cost segment have adopted enabling technology. There are nine interviewees (MC-1, MC-7, MC-8, MC-9, MC-10, MC-13, MC-18, MC-24 and MC-26) who belong to the second category of enabling and critical technology. All interviewees shared the same understanding that investments in technologies can help them sustain their current low cost advantage and possibly even low costs in the future. MC-8 opined that:

> "What was not possible in the past is made possible and faster now in the present."

MC-8 was referring to the purchase of manufacturing technologies which consist of pre-stressed and pre-cast building components. In the past, building components have to be cast in-situ on site. However, with the present automated assembly in prefabrication technology, it has subsequently allowed for cost reductions in terms of wastage and time savings and. at the same time, provides room for quality improvements. Furthermore, technology has also supported the firm's infrastructure, linking various computer applications from the manufacturing plants to head office and to the construction site. This deepened the vertical linkages and resulted in higher cost savings for the firm. The result coincides with the findings of Porter's (1998, 2004), whereby technological impact do not happen in isolation so much so that even one choice of technology too can have a pervasive impact throughout the value chain. This choice of technology is similar to the strategy adopted by MC-9, MC-10, MC-24 and MC-26, who have invested in special modular false-work systems, development of building services, fabrication of architectural components, and manufacture of structural works respectively. In addition, MC-9 also introduced the "Biometrics based Time-in Attendance System" to prevent unauthorized personnel from entering the worksite. In this context, the digital records also helped the firm to compute daily wages for its own staff which is said to have greatly improved productivity by allowing the firm then to focus on its deliverables to the clients. Two (MC-8 and MC-10) of the five interviewees have reported better financial performance after the incorporation of these technologies into the value chain. Technology has helped to facilitate the process of consolidating isolated activities, giving stakeholders a more comprehensive overview of their business operations. MC-10 said that:

> "We were able to gain better control over our operations, particularly the processes involved. We were able to offer a more competitive price."

Another plausible explanation could be attributed to the reduced bargaining power of the suppliers as suggested by Porter (1998, 2004), because the firms are able to manufacture and supply their very own building components and services. Although MC-9 has not yet reaped the benefits of the investments made by his firm, the general manager remains optimistic that this will not deter his firm from making further technological investments. MC-24 was unable to comment on this issue, as the matter is handled by the finance department while MC-26 was not willing to comment on such a sensitive issue.

Although it appears at this juncture that all the firms in this segment are competing with low costs, there is one particular firm (MC-1) who seems to be breaking away from the low cost strategy into the hybrid strategy. The upper management of the firm anticipated that the future construction landscape in Singapore will shift towards sustainability in response to global climate change. With this in mind, they are already investing and exploring the use of green technology, for example, through the use of bio-fuels as a substitute for electricity in private housing projects. For a start, the firm has already achieved the Green Mark status for two of their building projects, awarded by the Building and Construction Authority in Singapore. MC-1 was equally optimistic and encouraged about the future and hoped to gain more profitability in the industry. The executive director explained that:

> "We are on the right track with our investments and seeing the current business climate had spurred us to discover a new niche in the industry in the years to come."

In this context, it appears that firms in the low cost segment do have the capacities to invest in new and better technologies as compared to firms in the first category. However, it seems that there is an artificial barrier that discourages most of the firms from investing more than what they are currently doing. It seems that the lack of financial capabilities and the high risk exposure are yet again the primary concerns amongst the interviewees. MC-13 commented that:

> "Our profit margins are 3 to 5 % and yet total liability of one project is 10%."

As a result, all the interviewees (MC-1, MC-7, MC-8, MC-9, MC-10, MC-13, MC-18, MC-24 and MC-26) in the second category generally recognized their lack of technological investments when comparisons are made between them and firms in the third category. However, given the nature of the construction industry, they do not believe that developing new technologies i.e. proprietary technologies will greatly help to enhance the performance of their firms. MC-18 mentioned that:

> "Construction projects, on their own, are unique; hence it would be more practical for us to learn from project to project."

A majority of the interviewees shared the practical opinion of MC-18 in that the accumulation of project experiences will place them in a better position than the development of new technologies, through ways of limiting their risk exposure and anticipating the likelihood of problems occurring. The preference of the interviewees is in line with Porter's (1998, 2004) studies that learning through the accumulation of numerous small improvements can sometimes be more superior to major breakthroughs. This implies that the use of "new technology" may not be as useful because most of the interviewees felt strongly that project learning is more practical, safer, efficient and less costly. Similarly, like the rest of the interviewees, MC-7 felt that there is a lack of effective application across all types of projects which led to him explaining that:

> "Technologies used in the construction industry are not nano-technology where you can repeatedly use on a mass scale and still improve the performance of the product. In construction, every project has its own characteristics and risks to be taken into account. You cannot repeatedly use the same type of technology over and over again."

While all the interviewees understood the superiority and role of technologies used in differentiation, it is not always a rosy picture when it comes to technology for firms in this category. In pointing out the limitation of such technology, MC-10 noted that:

> "The technologies they used are so expensive, in order to pay for the money they have invested in, many a times these firms always have to change their clients' designs to suit their technology."

The comment of MC-10 can be interpreted as recognition of the drawbacks on the use of such technologies where he saw the inappropriateness of changing clients' designs and thought that firms should be more accommodating instead. A possible explanation for such a mindset could be the limited range of technologies possessed by MC-10 that had restricted the role of his firm in the design and planning stage. Studies by Dulaimi et al (2002) have shown that the early involvement of the main contractor in the project can derive more cost savings and client's satisfaction in terms of facilitating the construction processes, through innovative designs to increase the constructability of the project. In response to the comment of MC-10, MC-6 pointed out that his firm is selective of the type of projects and will only consider those that can showcase the abilities of his firm and exploit the full use of its technologies, in order to be answerable to the clients who are supposed to be paying a premium price for the services provided by his firm.

Another factor that five interviewees (MC-9, MC-13, MC-18, MC-24 and MC-26) commonly voiced out is related to the difficulty in forming long term partnerships with the industry players, especially joint ventures. MC-13 commented that:

> "No one is keen to form a long term relationship with us, perhaps because we are in the lower rung of the industry."

In addition, MC-26 speculated that the prime reason for this is probably due to the fact that potential joint venture partners believed that they do not stand to gain any benefits by partnering these firms. This is because many firms in the industry still do not have a good impression of firms in the low cost segment, stigmatizing firms competing in this segment to be "low quality and cheap", as highlighted by MC-9. The experiences of the interviewees suggest that the prevalence of price cutting in the past had created negative repercussions in the construction industry in Singapore, putting the low cost strategy firms at a disadvantage in so far as forming joint ventures to facilitate technology transfer and shared learning with one another is concerned. Furthermore, MC-24 pointed out that the Asian way of doing businesses does not seem to facilitate joint ventures among local firms themselves and yet ironically it is possible for local firms to enter into joint ventures with foreign firms. This surfaces the issue relating to the lack of a cooperative attitude among local firms. MC-24 explained that:

> "We have too much pride; everyone is their own bosses in their firms. Joint ventures will bring about problems like who is to lead the joint ventures? Everyone wants to be the leader. I think we are all too used to working with ourselves and not for others."

In this context, there appears to be two alternatives available for the Singapore construction industry. The industry players can welcome and embrace the notion of joint ventures and partnership, both working towards creating constructive and long term relationships, which can vastly improve efficiency and reduce conflicts (Construction 21 Steering Committee, 1999). Alternatively, the industry can continue to feel increasingly threatened by one another and begin to retreat into fortresses, stifling economic growth of the industry in the process.

By and large, the interviewees noted above used none of the critical technology in the third category. Hence, this has almost certainly created some misgivings over the employment of used and modified technologies, seeing that these technologies are easily imitated. The question lies in whether it is possible for firms in these two categories to gain certain competitive advantage over their rivals. However, Porter (1998, 2004) argued that the sustainability of a firm's strategy does not rest solely on how the technology is perceived to be unique and most importantly, not any and every technology is perceived to be good. Furthermore, Porter (1998, 2004) explained that modest improvements along the value chain have more merits for competitive advantage. Hence, the incorporation of technology is crucial only if used for its own sake. Thus, as described in the earlier sections, where despite not using "cutting edge" technology like firms in the third category, the interviewees are still able to achieve competitive advantage by exploiting their existing technologies and value chain, rather than developing technology in isolation. From this observation, it appears that the industry structure has tolerated the presence of non-pioneering technologies due to the variety of buyers with their different needs and demands.

Technology and differentiation

Seven interviewees (MC-3, MC-4, MC-5, MC-6, MC-16, MC-17 and MC-27) were involved with the differentiation strategy. However, with the exception of MC-4 who invested and utilized enabling technologies in the first category, the rest of the six interviewees have utilized and invested either in the second or third category. This is in stark contrast to the earlier observations, where no firms in the low cost strategy were found in the third category and only one of the differentiating firms was found in the first category.

All the seven interviewees (except MC-4) found technology to be critical partly because they are sustaining their competitive advantage on the premise of being unique. They mentioned the significant function of technology and MC-3 in particular opined that:

"Being unique and exclusive is our business."

Notwithstanding the similar differentiation segment, broad and focus differentiators adopted different forms and levels of technology to create and sustain their own unique competitive advantage.

With MC-6 and MC-27 being broad differentiators in the Singapore construction industry, both interviewees explained the importance and value of incorporating technology throughout their value chains to achieve their desired competitive advantage. With this in mind, both firms have made different policy choices to nurture such a diverse range of technology that pervades throughout their value chains, from primary to secondary activities, from firm infrastructure to procurement and from inbound logistics to service. MC-6 explained that:

> "Construction capabilities are our pride. The project team customized and put together all the planning and feeding the entire pre-construction to construction then maintenance, involving our equipment manufacturers, designers, engineers, to achieve a genuine synergistic effort."

As a result of such wide capabilities, both MC-6 and MC-27 are able to provide one-stop shop type of services to their clients who appreciate and incorporate concepts like life cycle costing in their projects or non-conventional procurement modes like turnkey, design and build, build-operate-transfer or public-private partnerships. Therefore, with the aid of technology, these two firms are in a favorable position with respect to how technology is employed to perform all the various activities in non-conventional procurement systems in Singapore. In addition, being technologically advanced itself is not sufficient to overcome the cost of differentiation. It will be ideal to exploit the full use of technology so that it can lead to further uniqueness. In the case of MC-27, the interviewee mentioned that the way one activity performed can affect the performance of the other activities along the value chain. MC-27 explained that:

> "By organic synergy, we generate through the unity of people and the different divisions within the organization that we are able to offer creative solutions to all our projects."

Thus, the results achieved through such linkages appear to align well with the Porter's (1998, 2004) argument, where the coordination of channels among the divisions within the firm can frequently result in uniqueness. On the other hand, MC-6 placed emphasis on the activity of continuous learning and reduce the effects of spillover learning to competitors which may lead to the erosion of differentiation through imitation. Hence, both interviewees deliberately added costs when searching to sustain their current competitive advantage; by having their own in-house research and development department as well as researchers and engineers to constantly work on improving existing products and solutions or creating new ones.

However, with the broad and focus differentiation strategies, firms (MC-3, MC-4, MC-5, MC-16 and MC-17) in this focus segment appeared to serve a smaller cluster of buyers. All interviewees, except MC-4, indicated that they did not pursue a diverse range of technologies. Instead, a dominant intensity in one or several of the support areas are chosen and implemented. Furthermore, not all firms pursue the same type of technology as they have to take into consideration of the product-buyer market scope. The decisions of these interviewees are in line with those of Porter's (1998, 2004) and Wright's (1996) findings, as the choice of technology reflects the various levels of "functional mix intensities". For example, research and development (MC-3's own brand of technology used in construction methodology and MC-5's advanced construction technology on the development of materials such as ultra strength concrete), purchasing (MC-5's electronic procurement system where all pre-tender information is stored for it to be transferred seamlessly to the post-tender stage and where this information can also be shared among parties within the firm, including those who are not involved with the project), communications (MC-16 stressed on the excellent coordination and sequencing between different trades and subcontractors since the firm does not undertake any of the construction works) and multi-disciplinary designs (MC-17's expertise in turnkey and engineering jobs together with the capacity to improve designs with the relevant designers to suit the entire construction process). In many ways, the attitude of the interviewees towards the use of technology is encouraging as it has helped them to improve their competitive positions in the industry and not just merely the cost of performance of each individual activity.

Reiterating what was suggested above, the differentiation - focus strategies were also used for competitive reasons. MC-17 explained the differences in technological strategies among the firms in the same focus group:

> "Although we are in the focus segment, we are still different in terms of the types of projects and clients we look for."

MC-3 shared the same opinion and mentioned that his firm does not feel the same amount of pressure in comparison to firms in the low cost strategy, who constantly outbid one another for projects. This may pose a grave problem in the long run. MC-3 claimed that his firm will follow up on projects that will allow the firm to demonstrate its core competencies, so as to avoid any of the unnecessary risks encountered. Generally, a majority of the interviewees stayed within their sector of expertise because of their familiarity and solid rapport with their clients within a particular sector. As a result, such competitive position places them in a better position to charge a premium for the price of differentiation, while not suffering from the aftermath of competitive pricing.

As noted above, differentiation firms indeed have the financial abilities as well as a pool of technical expertise to sustain their respective competitive advantage. However, MC-16 felt the strain of having to support the construction industry as it is apparent that there are still a number of firms who are still lagging behind in the area of technology and building expertise. He criticized not only the main contractors who are lagging behind, but also the subcontractors since the latter are the ones who carry out most of the works on the construction site. This underscores the importance of establishing a solid foundation for technology at the macro level for the entire construction industry and not just to pin-point the problem at the main contractors alone.

However, unlike the rest of the interviewees, MC-4 was not able to see eye to eye with how the use of technology can aid his firm in producing quality buildings and was satisfied with the way things were. He explained that:

> "The workmanship of the workers is more important than technology. Technology cannot do the workers' work, whereas workers can do the work of technology."

The reason for the low emphasis on technology is that MC-4 is only involved with small scale private residential projects which require more manual labor than the use of technology. Moreover, the mind-set of MC-4 towards technology appears to fit exactly into how the industry as a whole still lacks the inertia to embrace technology.

Generally, interviewees who have adopted moderately high levels of technology possibly reflect their strong financial capacities to do so. They also selected suitable projects than to take on all business offers that come along their way.

Technology and Hybrid Strategies

Four interviewees (MC-2, MC-19, MC-20 and MC-22) engaged themselves in using the hybrid strategy. Their common approach towards technology is made up of relatively high product and process research and development expenses which have led them to achieve low overall costs and high quality standards concurrently. To a large extent, technology makes it possible for them to switch between segments as competing using the hybrid strategy was not their initial intentions. This explains why all the four interviewees have transcended from their existing low cost segment into a more differentiated strategy. MC-19 opined that:

> "We were cutting, cutting, but you can only go so far, we got so bottom line oriented that it was inhibiting our growth."

In MC-19's opinion, the low cost strategy adopted by his firm was overwhelmed by plunging tender prices thus prohibiting the growth of his firm and with that, the firm concluded its presence in the low cost segment. MC-19 began to emphasize on their process research and development to enhance the differentiation of his firm through inbound logistics and technological change in operations. For example, extensive research and development in materials and operations technology have not only resulted in reducing its construction work sludge by 40 percent but also has a ripple effect on the environment and other related cost factors such as the amount of carbon emissions, diesel, labor, and transportation costs.

While the technology base of MC-19 is more focused on the secondary activities within the value chain, MC-20 placed more emphasis on primary activities by promoting "cluster inter-division synergies" and so allowed smaller unit to leverage on the group's strengths. The creation of separate divisions from procurement, cost control, engineering and maintenance have allowed the firm to move away from the traditional low cost design and bid procurement to other types of procurement like design-and-build, and turnkey which allowed the design responsibility to rest entirely with the contractor from the client. In this context, a more cost effective and yet innovative design can be made possible through the interaction of multi-disciplinary parties engaged by the contractor. Furthermore, MC-20 credited the success of technology to the joint venture agreements with leading foreign specialist firms. They not only benefited from the knowledge and expertise gained from witnessing first-hand the technology but more importantly, this has encouraged the firm to embrace technology more readily. MC-20 further added that:

> "We assure the clients to receive the quality that is commensurate with their expectations and the comfortable costs and schedule guarantees."

It appears plausible here that there are advantages with joint ventures, because relying on in-house abilities is rarely sufficient, especially with the rapid rate of knowledge growth and learning diffusion. Joint ventures with reputable construction-related firms can bolster the technical expertise of a firm. Moreover, the actual witnessing of how technology worked can also persuade firms to invest more capital into technology. This is especially so for firms in the low cost segment who may find it difficult to improve their competitive positions due to their inabilities to joint venture with other firms.

Two interviewees (MC-19 and MC-20) have engaged in a wide spectrum of projects from both the public sector and private sector that ranged from residential, commercial, industrial, institutional and recreational works, gradually widening their market share to enjoy cost savings. The versatility of their technologies on achieving economies of scales and bulk purchases has in turn allowed them to compete on a low cost strategy. MC-19 felt that the use of technology has helped to speed up the work processes, where all the subcontractors are able to work in a timely fashion without one intruding, delaying or interrupting another. MC-19 recalled the massive amount of work that had to be aborted and the "inevitable" poor quality work due to poor coordination, and explained that those were the times when there were no proper systems in place to coordinate and implement activities in an orderly manner.

Based on the anecdotes provided above by the interviewees, it appears that differentiation can also be a strategy for achieving low cost position, where the greater use of technology has placed them into a more favorable strategic position in comparison to their rivals highlighted earlier. Their abilities to invest in technology have also brought these firms to a position of high mobility where they are able to cut across the different strategic groups to compete for different projects. This is in contrast to differentiating firms, who are unable to compete in the low cost segment with their expensive technology and vice versa for the low cost firms. This is especially so in the competition for public residential housing projects, where the interviewees observed that public housing is becoming more sophisticated with added condominium-like features and where the quality demanded from these projects will definitely be higher than the past and current public housing projects in Singapore. This observation accords well with findings presented by Gann (1996) where there are escalating pressure from clients to improve quality as well as reduce costs and duration of projects. Nevertheless, the interviewees were very confident to deliver the expected quality standards with affordable costs, putting them in a good stead in the future for such projects.

While MC-19 and MC-20 were broad differentiators, MC-22 indicated the preference of his firm to stay within a niche sector where it will mostly handle repeat orders from the same client. The firm not only utilizes advanced construction technology as well as computer systems which facilitate a less costly and smoother operation process by supporting the need for timely operational reporting, scheduling and implementation. In addition, MC-22 was also looking at the potential of technology to formulate a "securitization scheme", to provide leasing support to his clients during the construction and operation stage. MC-22 explained that:

> "We are familiar with our clients that we know what they want and now we want to take that step further."

Similar to the other two interviewees highlighted earlier, they have used technology to differentiate themselves, but also at the same time reduced their overall total costs. Both MC-19 and MC-20 have succeeded in creating extra value added activities to provide a one-stop shop type of service to their clients, albeit one that is less costlier than their differentiating competitors. MC-22 adopted a different approach to create value for his clients by being involved with the clients' value chain through the sourcing of potential tenants and investors. This practice aligns well with Porter's (1998, 2004) observations, where the configuration of activities undertaken by MC-22 interacted with some of the activities of his clients that can perhaps help to lower the clients' costs without sourcing for a third party or raise their clients' performance by constructing a facility that can perform flexible functions for potential tenants and investors. Likewise, this practice is in line with Porter's (1998, 2004) assertion that differentiation can originate from creating value for the clients through the involvement of MC-22 along the clients' value chains.

Overall, the preferences of the interviewees relating to their choice of technologies were none like the interviewees in the differentiation segments where critical technologies like proprietary technologies were used. Thus, this does not seem to accord well with Porter's (1998, 2004) last condition for hybrid firms to thrive in the industry and that none of the interviewees take on a technological leadership position. Instead, all of them bought "used and tried technologies". However, the observations of the larger firms in the construction industry in Singapore appear to match the findings of Miller's (1992) studies, where hybrid strategies are still feasible in the absence of the above three exceptional conditions.

Technology has indeed played a major role in achieving both low cost and differentiation strategies, but all three interviewees mentioned the difficulties in affording their technologies. Apart from the difficulties mentioned, the interviewees also lamented at the lack of government support in terms of financial support and public awareness. MC-22 explained that:

> "High technology sector such as the health sciences and banking sectors received favorable support from the government; these sectors represent the focus of the nation and our sector is not as lucrative as others. Therefore, it is not fair to say that the construction sector is low technology, because if we have the same amount of support from the government, then it will be a different story."

Furthermore, the interviewees also indicated that bureaucratic red tape is one of the common hindrances for them to apply for public assistance schemes and incentives. In addition, another problem seems to have surfaced. MC-19 remarked that some of the schemes were designed by civil servants who appear to lack a rudimentary understanding of practices in the construction industry. This has defeated the purpose when certain schemes are completely ineffective in the context where technologies need to be bought and used, then proven to be efficient (measured by a certain percentage), before the firms can qualify for the financial support. As a result, such schemes do not help the firms at all because the element of risk is not reduced. The outcome of this, as portrayed in the study completed by Dulaimi et al (2002), is that the government has to take on a larger role in terms of providing the incentives as well as establishing government sponsored entities to pave the way for research and development efforts in the industry. This hints that the firms are not well positioned to carry out such large scale research and development activities on their own.

From the above observations, it appears that the experiences of the interviewees suggest that technological leadership towards the development of critical technologies will not be possible in the near future, predominantly in the low cost and hybrid segments, unless the government steps in to assume a bigger role and intervenes by taking the initiative to lead the industry's technological development efforts.

OBSERVATIONS

In this chapter, Porter's (1998, 2004) generic business strategies were identified among construction firms in Singapore. A number of these firms were found to be implementing non-generic strategies. These findings generally support the notion that hybrid strategies are viable and also as successful as the pure generic strategies. This seems to refute Porter's (1998, 2004) argument about the exclusivity of the generic strategies. The implication of this finding is that the industry structure should not be taken to be as simplistic as what Porter (1998, 2004) appeared to has done. Instead, there should be an acceptance of a myriad of strategies that may deviate from the pure generic strategies.

The findings also showed that buyers are gradually becoming more demanding and making more sophisticated choices. While price still remain a concern, there are other considerations such as quality, life cycle costing, service quality and time that are taken into their bidding and tendering criteria for evaluation. Thus, it is important for the construction industry in Singapore to carry on from here and not to revert back to its old ways of notorious price competition and under-cutting as this will place the industry in a position worse off than ever before. Given the changing demands of clients, it is surprising to observe that the role of research and development did not stand out as prominently even though many firms are able to make many small incremental steps to improve their current technology that surpass the actual benefits of research and development.

Chapter 8

CASE STUDY

BACKGROUND OF CASE STUDY

The case study firm presented in this chapter is the Singapore branch of a giant conglomerate that was set up in the mid-1980s to build one of the earliest Mass Rapid Transit (MRT) train station in Singapore. The branch gradually became the main contractor (MC-2) for building projects and has since been recognized in the Singapore construction industry as a reliable and innovative contractor. The firm was certified to ISO 9001, ISO 14001 and OHSAS 18001 standards relating to quality, environment as well as occupational health and safety. At the time of this study, the firm employed slightly more than 200 non-technical staff and 600 foreign workers. It has a large portfolio of prestigious and iconic projects, including high end luxurious condominiums, commercial buildings and mixed development projects in Singapore. A majority of its clientele are from the private sector.

COMPETITIVE ADVANTAGE

Within the context of Porter's (1998, 2004) propositions relating to the exclusivity of the generic strategies, MC-2 is also an exceptional case that does not fall under Porter's (1998, 2004) definition of competitive advantage. The firm was observed to possess a hybrid strategy of cost advantage and differentiation in the focus segment. This was made possible with support from its management systems, strong commitments to its staff and staunch beliefs in innovative and creative solutions through the use of technology. The following sections shall further elaborate how MC-2 was able to achieve cost advantage and differentiation simultaneously in the focus segment of the construction industry in Singapore.

Cost Advantage

Control Cost Drivers

MC-2 gained cost advantage through the control of cost drivers by paying attention to the elements in its value chain. In the following sections, it can be seen that the firm's cost advantage position was derived from multiple sources within the value chain.

Economies of Scale

MC-2 owned a proprietary metal formwork system for mechanized construction that makes it extremely economical and efficient, when working on large scale projects. This is because the formwork system was uniquely designed for high rise buildings that are not possible for the smaller projects. Moreover, the firm also introduced efficient and complementary concrete designs to suit the functionality of the formwork system. In order to maximize the use of their formwork system, the firm is very selective in considering the suitability of the projects it undertakes. In this context, procurement systems such as Design-and-Build and Public Private Partnerships would allow the contractor to exercise control over the design aspects of the building, thus helping the firm to realize the full benefits of its formwork system. This unique formwork system not only gives rise to cost savings but is also known for its capacity to significantly reduce completion time. This was pointed out by the project director of MC-2 who explained that:

> "We are able to cut the completion time by one year (to certain projects) against the initial construction schedule set by our clients, because of our formwork system that has one of the shortest cycle time in the industry."

The use of this system formwork also produces a high quality external finish, thus eliminating laborious cement rendering works that save on both time and cost. In fact, a thin skim coat suffices to achieve a good finish before painting. The formwork technology used by MC-2 appears to have accentuated the cost advantage for the firm in the long run through the development of such low cost processes.

Management of the Learning Curve and Keep Learning Exclusive

The firm understood that its employees are its main asset in helping the firm to grow and to keep abreast of new and current practices in the construction industry. According to the project director, the benefits reaped from investments in employee career development are realized in two to five years time. Hence, the plan is to retain its employees by making the firm more attractive for the employees than its competitors. Furthermore, MC-2 has its own pool of foreign workers and supervisors who have been fully trained. This helps the firm to save costs and control the quality of building construction.

Enhance Bargaining Leverage through Purchasing Policies and Selection of Appropriate Suppliers

The construction industry is considered to be one of the largest consumers of raw materials. MC-2 recognized that procurement of materials is an essential tool that can greatly affect costs. Hence, a separate procurement division was created within the group as well as on every project site. At the macro level, its parent group appointed purchasing executives who are responsible for procuring different types of materials around the world. The project director explained that:

"This exclusive group of people travels around the world solely to search for suitable materials for the group's diverse range of projects."

This shared approach to procurement lowers the costs of purchasing premium quality components for its projects in Singapore. In addition, taking into account of the weakening US dollar for hedging purposes, the firm strategizes on what currencies to keep and to sell as this is extremely vital to importing materials from overseas. As a result of cost discounts being achieved in view of the weakening US dollar, especially when their subcontractors are asking to be paid in Euro currencies instead of the US dollar, the project director explained that:

"We need to plan and think ahead in order to minimize our risks. The firm monitored the market fluctuations. Then we make decisions like keeping the currency when the price is down or buying more Euro dollars when the US dollar is showing signs of weaknesses."

At the micro level, a procurement department is established on the construction site which consists of a procurement manager and a team of quantity surveyors who will analyze and decide on the most suitable materials for their projects. Moreover, the purchasing strategy of MC-2 relies heavily on long term partnerships with its suppliers, for instance through pre-bid agreements. The project director explained that the separation of the department allows the employees to be focused on procurement activities alone and not be pre-occupied by other activities such as monthly progress payments for subcontractors and payment forecasts. This is so that they can gain insights into how unit costs may be lowered by analyzing the unit costs of the purchased inputs collectively as a group.

The Indonesian government imposed a sudden ban on sand exports to Singapore in early 2007. Despite having good relations with its suppliers, MC-2 was however not spared from suffering the full impact of the sudden ban on sand exports to Singapore. In this context, suppliers have refused to abide by the original terms of contract, leaving MC-2 with a limited supply of sand and thus stalling the progress of its projects. In addition, all the suppliers also demanded cash upon the delivery of the sand supplies. This explains why the sudden sand ban had severely affected the cash flow and profit margins of MC-2. In order to mitigate the losses incurred, the firm has to depend on *ex gratia* payments by its clients because the occurrence of the sand ban was not construed as *force majeure,* which if it was the case, would release the parties from performing their remaining obligations under the contract. Hence, contractually, the firm has to be fully liable for the additional costs incurred for its private sector building projects. This is in contrast to the public sector projects where the Singapore government would shoulder up to 75 percent of the increase in prices of sand and granite to assist construction firms tide over such difficult times.

However, in view of the inflationary pressures on material prices (excluding sand), MC-2 tried to mitigate the adverse impact by procuring the materials much earlier than usual. This means that its future subcontract packages will be awarded earlier so that the prices are "locked in" or hedged. In this context, for example, packages for architectural work will be awarded earlier in the early structural work stage of a project. Nonetheless, the project director is fully aware that there are risks in locking in prices early. However, these are risks that he was prepared to take. In his opinion, prices are likely to escalate over the next six months at the time of this study because of the introduction of mega projects such as the two integrated resorts in Marina Bay and Sentosa Island. Hence by doing so, this would place the firm in a favorably low risk position.

Exploit Cost Linkages within the Value Chain

The project director stressed that attention should be directed towards the subcontractors and their material supplies:

> "What were out of our control were the subcontractors. If they go burst then the whole project will suffer serious damage."

To avoid the risk of project stoppage and the hassle of re-tendering, MC-2 will usually help the subcontractors purchase their materials because many of them are small sized enterprises who generally cannot afford to undertake such financial liabilities. The project director pointed out that:

> "Many of the subcontractors here are very small in size. They cannot absorb so much risk and therefore this is where we can play a part."

For instance, in one of its project, MC-2 found a novel way of lowering the costs of production for its tiling subcontractor, by laying tiles without the use of screed. The technique relies on the use of good quality concrete. Hence, MC-2 provided the concrete and tiles, while the subcontractor provided the skilled workforce for the job. With this arrangement and method of working, a tremendous amount of time, material costs and manpower were saved. This highlights the importance of linkages within the construction value chain, and that no matter how minor the activities may seem to be, these can still have an exponential effect on the building project as a whole.

There are also many other linkages which MC-2 had identified and exploited to the best advantage of the firm. Firstly, there is a cost control division in the construction site. This is managed by a cost controller who is responsible for all matters relating to cash inflows and outflows such as progress payments, monitoring of materials ordered, employees' salaries, compilation of weekly budgetary reports, and so on, so that all monies expended or received are accounted for. The project director explained the necessity for strict cost control:

> "We know what we spent on, from stationary to raw materials. We will know which department is the most wasteful, especially if there is excessive abortive work done by our engineers. This was because when our procurement department placed an order, it is always the exact amount, no more, no less."

In relation to cost control, the firm has also adopted an innovative concept for controlling costs – through the mechanism for target cost incentive. This concept is however more applicable for the larger projects. A sum will be agreed upon between MC-2 and its clients for defined potential changes. Therefore, whatever remains unspent upon completion of the contract is shared equally between both parties. For this concept to be fully effective, the project director however explained that:

> "Partnering and open communication between them and their client were mandatory and this should be the way how future businesses should work, encouraging contractors to be more pro-active."

Secondly, the architectural drawings are integrated with the structural drawings to facilitate communication between different parties. The integration of these two sets of drawings will help to improve the productivity of the entire value chain, from the quantity surveyors who have to do the taking-off of quantities to the engineers who have to communicate to the workers on site for action.

Working with Subcontractors to Exploit Vertical Linkages

The practice to develop proper partnerships with the subcontractors has become a norm in the firm's selection process; the project director said that in every trade, the firm has its own "preferred subcontractors". The selection criteria are based on the track records and previous working relationships with the subcontractors. These preferred subcontractors are used to offset risks, such as those relating to the quality of building, improvements in productivity and time saved during the period when the tender is being called. The project director highlighted that the additional costs for selecting preferred subcontractors are compensated by a reduction in the number of inspection needed in the finished product:

> "We cannot be so short-sighted as to select subcontractors who were the lowest, as the lowest might not translate into reality. Instead, it should be based on good working relationships where both parties already knew how each other work. Hence, the subcontractors required less supervision from us and yet quality was achieved. Therefore, despite paying a bit more upfront, there were some hidden cost savings."

In line with the responses of the other interviewees highlighted earlier, the program director also drew attention to the human factor which is often the hardest to coordinate. This is where he has to make sure that all parties can work together harmoniously. This observation indicates that the nature of construction not only entails the technical aspects but also involves a series of interactive and interpersonal issues relating to multidisciplinary teamwork.

Differentiation

Differentiation and the Value Chain

Differentiation would be what sets a firm apart from the rest and this can be done in any part of the value chain. MC-2's driver of uniqueness stems from its approach to quality that goes beyond certification, in which imbues all areas of its business: its management system, its people and its workmanship. Hence, this approach reflects the firm's conviction that quality is the key to being competitive and is the best way for it to satisfy its clients better than its competitors.

The procurement of raw materials and other inputs has a considerable impact on the performance of the end product. As a result, the procurement of resources is a major driver of uniqueness for MC-2. For example, the specialized procurement department within the group pays particular attention to the quality of the materials vis-à-vis the cost and how they will enhance the performance of the building. As the project director explained:

> "Do not look at the initial costs of materials but see what they can do beyond that. In many cases, they had longer life span than the cheaper materials. Thus, this is translated into lower servicing cost in the long term for the client."

MC-2 progressed to such an extent along this route that the firm even acquired its glass façade supplier who went into financial difficulties and was unable to fulfill their contractual obligations. After the acquisition, MC-2 took over the role of the glass façade supplier and this produced positive implications, such as low defects rates, attractive product appearances, increased buyer's performance and lower costs.

Other successful differentiators also created uniqueness in the support activities of MC-2 whereby the firm's expertise did not rest on purely construction activities alone. Instead it encompasses financing, design, building, operations and maintenance. The firm has also started developing its expertise in the fields of electrical and maintenance works (namely in electrical, mechanical and thermal engineering as well as facilities management) to provide the firm with business activities that have complementary business cycle that lead to the creation of recurrent income. The project director was confident that with the added technical expertise, the firm can further provide a more comprehensive package of technology and service offering for its clients. MC-2 hoped to become a major player in Public-Private Partnership (PPP) procurement in the construction industry by providing a suite of services which includes finance, design, construction, operations and maintenance of a facility.

Differentiation and Technology in the Value Chain

Research and innovation constitute the core strategy of the parent group as well as that of the firm's in helping to ensure that projects delivered are of the highest quality and at the same time, offering these at competitive prices. Hence, technology has played a vital role in the growth of the firm as well as in the formation of its strategic plans. In the case of MC-2, the results of its R&D programme did not add additional costs to its operations, which are quite unlike to what Porter (1998, 2004) has suggested. On the other hand, MC-2 has a similar framework to that of MC-22, which comprises of the Quality (Q), Safety (S) and Environment (E) thrusts. This framework involves six principal themes: sustainable construction, competitive cost approach, concrete research, reduction of noise and vibration, increasing the use of robotics to deal with productivity and difficult-to-perform tasks and building information management systems. Hence, differentiation will appear to be costly when firms need to deliberately invest more money in order to be unique. However, such conditions may be short-lived, as the outcome of the technology has improved the performance of materials and site equipment, safety and quality, optimization of lead times, and make certain jobs less arduous as well as reducing negative environmental impact.

With this in mind, MC-2 has not only successfully made its operations unique but also simultaneously offers its services at competitive costs In this context, MC-2 has a cost advantage in differentiating. Porter (1998, 2004) noted that such achievement is only made possible if the firm has accomplished significant innovation which competitors have not adopted (Porter, 1998, 2004). The approach adopted by MC-2 accords well with Porter's (1998, 2004) findings because the firm has introduced a number of engineering "firsts", including its metal formwork system. In addition, it is being seen that technology is such a powerful tool that MC-2 is able to use this to achieve the best of both worlds. The project director opined that:

> "Our technologies are advanced and original. Most of it were imported and used by our own people and not third parties, thus making it impossible to imitate."

This explains that the firm's sustainable competitive advantage hinges on its technological leadership as other firms have no access to such confidential information, making it impossible for them to replicate. Moreover, the firm is constantly innovating and improving on its existing technologies or creating new ones, possibly faster than the majority of the other firms in the construction industry. As a result, MC-2 has enjoyed the reputation in the construction industry as being a "reliable and efficient" player through the use of its technologies.

From the above observations, it appears that technology has indeed played an indispensable role in contributing to the differentiation strategies of MC-2. The following four categories encompass the technological strategies adopted by MC-2:

1. Engineering and works (methods, structure/tooling, design, etc).
2. IT (products, applications and services).
3. Management, finance and legal (cost control, accounting, project financing, etc).
4. Human resources (multimedia terminals, management programs, etc).

The four main categories above have also been translated into commitments, which in turn have resulted in concrete actions. Two such examples are described below.

Example 1: Whole-life Cycle Costing in Engineering and Construction Works

Other than developing prototype technologies which are closely related to the integration of costs and product quality, the parent company of MC-2 has also invested heavily in R&D projects that looked into whole-life costing. Every element such as concrete and floor coverings, for example, are closely examined and different technical options are compared in terms of the price of construction, price of maintenance, expected building life, costs of removal, costs of replacement and so on. Hence, building collectively on its parent's global capability, MC-2 has placed greater emphasis on introducing life cycle costing in its projects and to its clients. The importance of building in whole-life costing in the construction works has performed a pivotal role in creating value added services in its value chain, especially in Public Private Partnership or PPP procurement which is still in its infancy stage in Singapore. The project director explained that:

"It is within us and our responsibility to use higher specifications, products and materials that will cause less disruption to clients."

Example 2: Application of Computer System in IT and Human Resources

Since the core businesses of MC-2 focus on large and complex construction projects, the ability to assess project risks, design for optimal design solutions and determine suitable construction methodologies are the key reasons for the ongoing success of the firm in the construction industry. It is thus critical for the firm to count on past projects for client references and to gain valuable insights, including international projects among its different business units. This expertise and knowledge are stored, spread across its IT systems and shared within the know-how of the firm which is supported by a central computer system related to project planning documents, proposals, progress reports, memorandums and others. Furthermore, the project director explained that:

"Within the group and the firm, expertise and knowledge are constantly evolving. Therefore, there was a need for a system to integrate new skills and experience into the existing pool of expertise and knowledge."

This demonstrates the importance of connecting to knowledge and keeping abreast with new and more complex technologies because working on outdated information can have adverse commercial implications. Because of the connectivity as well as integration of activities and information, it also creates another source of differentiation through the coordination of linked activities such that better coordination of quotations, procurement and manufacturing schedule may lower inventory costs and at the same time shorten delivery time.

On the whole, it can be seen that the services the firm offers originate from not just one technology but several technologies that make the firm unique. In addition, the selection of the technologies reflect the firm's understanding of the local construction industry and its market structure, what activities to undertake as well as how it should go about conducting these activities.

Differentiation and the Buyer

The approach taken by MC-2 to satisfy the needs of its clients was seen earlier in the sections relating to cost advantage and differentiation. It is through these two sources of advantages that help the firm to gain client confidence and create its distinctive corporate image of being a genuinely quality class builder. This approach reveals that MC-2 is able to translate buildings in their physical tangible forms of good workmanship standards. The ability of MC-2 to deliver good quality not only helps its clients to raise their performance but also lower their direct and indirect costs. The project director emphasized that the success of any projects is to explore various avenues to increase the buyer's value as well.

As a result, MC-2 enjoys "exclusive rights" to serve the same client (denoted herein as Developer A), wherein MC-2 had constructed many repeat projects for Developer A. Along the same line of reasoning, the contracts agreed between the firm and Developer A are usually on a negotiated basis and this has helped the firm to address the critical question of profitability, where the firm is able to lower the buyer's purchasing power. Hence, this appears to demonstrate that MC-2 has widened the gap between the difference of what its clients are willing to afford and the costs attributed to MC-2 for carrying out these activities. In this context, MC-2 is involved in activities that affect profits.

Other than lowering buyer's costs or improving performance, the differentiation strategy of MC-2 has converted the buyer's incomplete knowledge into opportunities for competitive advantage. In the context of PPP which has recently been introduced by the Singapore government in the construction industry, MC-2's international exposure to such procurement had allowed the firm to capitalize on this new form of differentiation preemptively and educate its clients on the value of the PPP concept. For example, lowering the client's costs through life cycle costing where higher initial costs may spell a less costly operations and maintenance expenditure for the facility in the future. This is especially critical, because operations and maintenance works would occupy a significant fraction of the client's costs when the facility is transferred back into the hands of the client. Hence, the price premium that MC-2 commands had demonstrated both the actual value and the level to which the buyer perceives this value, i.e. meeting the signaling criteria of the client rather than providing mere tangible options which the client already recognizes. In addition, the project director advised that:

> "No matter how realistic our proposal is, our clients need to see the value that we are providing. This comes mainly from our solid reputation in Singapore where the value promised will be delivered to our clients."

INTERRELATIONSHIPS AMONG BUSINESS UNITS

Increasing economic and competitive developments were cited by the project director as the two main reasons that give rise to the importance of interrelationships. Such a difficult marketplace environment has made it increasingly important to consolidate businesses collectively to leverage on the strengths of the various business units within the parent group. This is especially so when global competition is at its best in an open economy like Singapore. In this context, MC-2 has been successful due to its ability to synergize with the capabilities of its parent group based outside Singapore, then exporting it back into the local environment in Singapore. The parent group makes this possible by creating mechanisms for sharing among the various business units, such that they prioritize the technology and R&D allocation according to the two following criteria: the potential for cross-company applications and the high added value potential. In other words, it focuses on developing technologies which have the most potential to permeate across the company and then feed information to all business units instead of using the technology in just one single business unit in isolation. This appears to reinforce Porter's (1998, 2004) suggestions where technology strategies can be strengthened at a corporate level. In this context, the key of the technology strategy is in the finding, exploiting and creating technological inter-relationships among business units (Porter, 1998, 2004).

Much attention has been given to identify and exploit these technologies in a systematic manner, particularly in the area of technological transfer which provides tangible opportunities to reduce costs and enhance differentiation along its value chain. Technologies are assimilated into many of its production processes, design development and procurement.

The growing sophistication of information technology and computer systems has facilitated the assimilation of technological transfer. The outcome of this has not only achieved lower costs and improved sustainable differentiation but also leads to time savings through better and faster decision-making by its employees worldwide. Furthermore, their employees can gain from the knowledge of the know-how to manage a particular type of activity simply by tapping into the group's vast capabilities, thus helping them to become more productive. For example, MC-2 has applied the necessary skills needed for its PPP project in Singapore as well as tapping onto the expertise of other business units in their PPP projects worldwide. By doing so, MC-2 has altered the landscape of competition by dramatically enhancing its competitive position in the Singapore construction industry.

For the reasons above, the business units across the group helped MC-2 sustain their competitive advantage due to exploitations of technological inter-relationships vis-à-vis their competitors. This synergy has elevated the ability of MC-2 to compete using the hybrid strategy in the context of the Singapore construction industry.

CONCLUSION

The success and sustainability of the hybrid strategy adopted by MC-2 depends on doing many things well, spanning across the entire value chain, where cost, differentiation, technology and interrelationships are involved. There are many different key drivers that come together, producing drivers of cost and uniqueness. In addition to this, the firm also emphasizes on understanding the values of its clients and the achievement of their business goals through customizing its strategies and recognizing market trends.

Chapter 9

CONCLUSION

RESTRUCTURING MEASURES IN POSITIVE ENVIRONMENT

It is worthwhile to note, from the empirical findings presented earlier, that there appears to be a preference for construction firms to move in the direction of differentiating themselves instead of competing head-on aggressively on low costs. This observation should also be interpreted in two vastly different market environments that firms may possibly face in the construction industry. In this context, the market environment may exude positive confidence or negative sentiments.

A study of how construction firms have fared in a positive business environment was completed by Low (1992) who also highlighted the measures adopted by construction firms to help ensure their survival when the building industry eventually slows down. In this context, survival measures fundamentally involve the minimization of expenditure and costs, and the maintenance of business viability and profitability. The survival measures planned ahead by construction firms in a positive business environment then prevalent in 1992 in Singapore, in anticipation of a slowdown in construction activities include the following.

Cost Cutting

The adoption of typical cost cutting measures to minimize wastages and unnecessary expenditures constitutes an important survival tactic for construction firms. Some construction firms have also suggested the freezing of salaries and further adjustments to wages as part of the overall cost cutting exercise (Low, 1992).

Intensify Attempts to Secure Jobs

As many building projects as possible should be secured to bridge over the slump period which, on average, is expected to last for two years. Construction firms should, however, need to exercise prudence in tender preparation as disputes which arise may further aggravate their financial positions. If viable, construction firms should first initiate in-house development projects by utilizing resources from their land bank, if any. This will not only help to maintain a backlog but also take advantage of the fall in prices of building materials and resources to achieve lower construction costs during the slump period.

Construction firms should also adhere strictly to their intended profit margins and secure jobs at that level. They should not tender below the intended profit margins as this may do them more harm than good. To do otherwise may spark off a vicious cycle in the industry when tender prices may continue to fall with intense competition from firms who habitually tender at or below costs to secure volume. Even firms with sound financial backing may become insolvent if they continue to operate below costs and when the slump in the industry persists. A large number of firms will then be weeded out and prices will begin to pick up again when competition between construction firms falls (Low, 1992).

Rationalization of Personnel

Construction firms have maintained that overheads can be minimized by keeping only the core personnel and utilizing them fully in their building projects (Low, 1992). This gradual measure can help to avoid retrenchment. Nevertheless, the firm should not overload its staff to the extent that costly mistakes, caused by work pressure, may need to be rectified. If necessary, additional staff can be employed on a contract or project basis. The performance of staff may also be maximized by motivating them to strive and collaborate through hard times.

Maintain Rapport with Developers

Although good rapport should be maintained with property developers, construction firms ought to be cautious of developers whom they are not fully familiar with. This is because some developers will take undue advantage of a highly competitive market to corner and press construction firms into further financial woes. Construction firms have highlighted that they would only tender for projects by developers whom they think are reliable and can be trusted (Low, 1992).

RESTRUCTURING MEASURES IN ADVERSE ENVIRONMENT

In a study of how construction firms have reacted to the Asian financial crisis in 1997, Low and Lim (1999) found that the restructuring measures taken by a majority of the construction firms include the following:

1. Continuous cuts in supplier costs
2. Direct sourcing from the suppliers
3. Encourage individual participation through quality circles
4. Introduce new methods of managerial control
5. Explain current difficulties faced to employees

A majority of the construction firms in the study conducted by Low and Lim (1999) also took up marketing options by speeding up project delivery and rectification works. The more popular cost-cutting measures include the following:

1. More competitive bidding for subcontracting works
2. Freezing salaries
3. Training staff to look for ways to cut costs
4. Cutting bonuses
5. Employing staff on a project basis
6. Cutting overtime work
7. Keeping only the core personnel

More than half of all the construction firms in the study completed by Low and Lim (1999) also adopted the following long-term strategies:

1. Establishing good relationships with sources of funds
2. Restructuring
3. Marketing
4. Avoiding speculation on inventories
5. Long-term financing
6. Turning to leasing equipment

Many construction firms also tried to establish a better rapport with developers and suppliers as well as improve staff morale to enhance productivity. Nonetheless, the above findings should be examined individually for all the construction firms. This is because the outlook of a firm's core area of business will differ from one core area to another and from one sector to another (Low, 1992; Penrose 1995). The core area of a firm may be centered on institutional works, industrial works, commercial works, civil engineering works and residential works. Each core area can, in turn, be in the public or private sector. It appears that construction firms are more likely to maintain or increase investments when the outlook of their core business is positive and when these firms perceive that there will be little or no difficulty in selling their assets when needed.

The study completed by Low and Lim (1999) only covered the strategic measures adopted by construction firms who were affected by the currency crisis, which first snowballed in July 1997 following the volatile fluctuations in several Asian currencies in what is now known as the 1997 Asian financial crisis. The strategic measures presented by Low and Lim (1999) should therefore be read within the context of the period from 1997-1998. At that point in time, no one knew for sure when the Asian financial crisis would end or would indeed degenerate further into a global crisis. Consequently, the strategies adopted or to be adopted by construction firms thereafter would obviously depend on how long the crisis was expected to last. The reformulation of strategic measures is therefore to be expected. Nonetheless, the analysis presented by Low and Lim (1999) provides a framework to better understand how construction firms strategized and in the process, also provided valuable strategic lessons for other construction firms to help tide them over the then 1997 Asian financial crisis.

SUMMARY OF CURRENT STUDY

While the Singapore construction industry is small, the market reflects its dynamism; judging by the presence of various strategic positions that the interviewees involved with the study held and shared with the research team. The market is identified as a difficult environment to compete in, given the turbulent surroundings with greater and more different expectations. The aims of the study seek to link the strategic performance of construction firms with Porter's (1998, 2004) generic business strategies, and in particular, to assess whether there are any discrepancies between Porter's (1998, 2004) theoretical framework and the responses of the participating construction firms as well as to examine how these are translatable into actual strategic performance.

The study began with a literature review as presented earlier. A brief background of Porter's (1998, 2004) concepts of competitive strategy and advantage were discussed and two dissimilar types of competitive advantages were identified and evaluated. The study also presented the possible responses of the construction firms in Singapore to the concepts proposed by Porter's (1998, 2004).

The research design was based on in-depth interviews. The questionnaire comprised open ended questions based on knowledge obtained from the literature review. Data were collected through face-to-face and e-mail interviews with 27 senior industry practitioners who had undertaken projects in Singapore from the year 1998 onwards. Interviews were conducted from the period of July through to December 2007 in the offices of the participating construction firms. The qualitative data were analyzed using the deductive approach and reported verbatim. These were related to the interviewees' responses and findings from the case study.

MAIN FINDINGS

The study found that not all construction firms adopted Porter's (1998, 2004) generic business strategies. Instead, there appears to be a handful of interviewees who have adopted either the hybrid strategy or no strategy at all. Not all firms are found to compete in the low cost segment. This implies a shift from the traditional cost-based pricing strategy to a more market based strategy. As markets become more globalized and with fiercer competition, competing for projects is no longer based solely on price alone. Hence, this gives rise to the presence of differentiating firms as well as the emergence of firms who have adopted the hybrid strategy.

Interestingly, the hybrid strategy competed on the basis of both low cost and differentiation which stresses the development of new or improved products for differentiation while achieving low cost. This strategy seems to provide more flexibility than that proposed by Porter's (1998, 2004). Hence, this appears to offer an alternative which can be more suitable for the future landscape in the Singapore construction industry; where the hybrid strategy will represent a combination between a low cost and differentiation strategy, allowing the firms in this cluster to compete using both strategies. In this context, it can also be difficult for firms to achieve a pure differentiation position in the construction industry and yet on the other hand, there can be a reluctance to revert to aggressive cost competition and price wars.

The first cluster of thirteen firms primarily competed on the basis of the low cost strategy and has the tendency to demonstrate an emphasis on low costs by focusing on their project expenditures such as low manufacturing expenses. However, they do have high capacity utilization, in the form of increasing their revenue by taking on more projects. Additionally, they have charged lower prices and eschewed product changes, as shown evidently by their low investments in technology.

The second cluster of seven differentiators has stressed the importance of technology and quality, as shown by their relatively higher investments in technology to develop improved or new products. They have justified their higher prices by meeting the needs of their clients owing to their unique products and services, thereby expressing a reduced concern for achieving the low cost position.

Despite the purported advantages of having at least one strategic position, there are two interviewees who have reported that their firms do not have clear strategic positions in the construction industry. This is because both firms are of the view that it is more appropriate to plan strategies in accordance with individual project characteristics.

Nevertheless, there is a majority of the firms which have noted the importance of examining related activities within their value chains, understanding the role of technology, and the inter-relationships among their different business units. The contributing factors that hinder these construction firms to invest in more technology are costs, the type of procurement systems and the perceived ineffectiveness of incentives provided by the government.

Notwithstanding the technical aspects of construction, human relations and partnerships are also regarded as critical factors which contribute to the performance of these construction firms. The study found that local firms are able to embrace technology more willingly when they form partnerships with their technologically more advanced peers by means of directly gaining the technological know-how through transfer.

CONTRIBUTION TO KNOWLEDGE AND PRACTICE

The findings in the study provide an in-depth insight into the various strategic profiles of large construction firms in the Singapore construction industry. These findings will in turn serve as a guide towards gaining a better understanding of the strategic intents of firms in the construction industry, and for construction firms to improve their performance in terms of cost, time, quality, client value and profitability.

The findings will benefit construction firms who are contemplating a review of their strategic intents in the industry, especially from the low cost to the differentiation or the hybrid domain. From the findings, these firms may steepen their learning curves and be better prepared by riding on the experiences of other construction firms. As for those firms that are already in other segments of the construction industry, they may use this platform to review the different approaches to managing strategies. The recommended practices below can be considered to steer the future potential growth and performances of firms.

RECOMMENDATIONS FOR COST ADVANTAGE

From the findings, a large number of firms are found to be in the cost advantage category and are unlikely to move out of this segment. It is recommended that firms need to better understand the behavior of costs (within their value chains and linkages) and exploit more opportunities to improve their relative strategic positions. Firms can devise their own cost control programs to monitor every value activity over time and among competitors. This should take place not only during construction. These programs should be created in such a way to avoid over-looking indirect or small-scale activities, and to avoid disregarding the importance of the interaction and exploitation of such linkages.

It is also recommended that firms adopt a partnering approach with other competent firms to reduce the element of risk. This will also help to improve their long-term commitments towards collaboration with other firms as well as to move towards the acceptance of investments in more technologies, rather than for short term profits.

Despite the uniqueness of the construction industry and the limited capacities of construction firms, such firms should avoid being "divers", resorting to suicidal bids so much so that they succumb to the pricing pressure and spiral downwards to reckless cost-cutting and price wars. Instead, their low cost strategies should genuinely reflect their abilities to examine and alter the various cost saving opportunities along the value chain, making it difficult for the competitors to imitate their cost positions.

RECOMMENDATIONS FOR DIFFERENTIATION

Given the uniqueness that characterized differentiating firms, it is recommended that differentiation should go beyond the physical products. Similar to the low cost cluster, firms should exploit opportunities to differentiate in all parts of the value chain, through measures of either making it harder for the competitors to imitate or introduce innovative schemes in the value chain with the aim of enjoying a lasting benefit from differentiation. Firms should adopt a more proactive stance when it comes to changing buyer or market circumstances instead of taking a back-seat. Change creates new opportunities for differentiation and can introduce clients to novel perspectives of viewing the products and services offered. Increased environmental consciousness globally, for example, has led to a greater awareness in minimizing carbon footprints in the environment. In this context, firms can re-invent themselves to ride on this new wave to explore the potential opportunities found in or derived from environmentally friendly construction practices and processes.

It is also important for firms to keep themselves relevant through a better understanding of their clients' value and not be too carried away by differentiation. In other words, firms must still keep costs at bay to their competitors because too much or unnecessary differentiation will render the firm vulnerable if the premiums are too high or when there are competitors who are able to correctly identify the right quality and provide services at lower prices. To reduce the susceptibility of firms to cost-oriented competitors, a successful differentiator should apply cost cutting measures to activities which have been rendered unimportant to the buyer, particularly when the price premium becomes too high.

RECOMMENDATIONS FOR HYBRID STRATEGIES

It has been recognized in the study that the pure differentiators are far too superior in technological abilities and that it takes a long learning curve for firms in this cluster to get there. It is recommended that they explore the area of niches according to the size and scale of these firms, where they can tailor themselves to meet the value chains of their clients and specialize in their respective segments. They should in fact respond more aggressively to the client's demands than firms in the pure differentiation segment. It will also benefit these firms should they decide to export their niche products and services overseas as a group of consortium eventually.

GENERAL RECOMMENDATIONS

All construction firms are recommended to think beyond into the long term because competitive advantage can help make strategies more concrete, more actionable and that can be better managed by selecting a particular configuration of products and services aligned to deliver a mix of activities to their chosen group of clients. Strategy is no longer just a broad vision for construction firms to follow but a group of defined activities that a firm has chosen compared to its competitors. In this manner, firms can put together a strategy that plays to their strengths and the way in which they implement the strategy.

From the above observations, it seems that a majority of the interviewees have, by and large, under-invested in technology capacity, resulting in low barriers of entry for newcomers into the industry. Bearing this in mind, firms ought not to limit their technology strategies merely to the role of "research and development" or "scientific breakthroughs", important though these may be. This must be widened to a larger scope. No matter how mundane the activities appear to be, technology does have the ability to alter industry boundaries; for instance, broaden the market scope and improve the performance of the firms through the products and services offered. In addition, minor but yet cumulative developments in many activities within the value chain can prove to be more sustainable than a major breakthrough that is readily detectable to industry players and eventually turn out to be an easy target to the detriment of the incumbent firm.

LIMITATION

The limitation faced relates to the sample of construction firms who have been studied within the context of a rapidly shifting and changing global economy. As an example, the study was completed shortly before the onslaught of the global financial meltdown caused by toxic housing assets that crippled the banking sector in the United States in 2008. For this reason, the strategies adopted by these construction firms will evolve in tandem with changes experienced in the global marketplace. It will therefore be desirable if more construction firms can be interviewed regularly as part of an on-going study so that the results can be updated frequently in line with eventful changes in the global economic and political platforms. Notwithstanding this backdrop, the study has successfully provided an in-depth insight into the respective strategic positions and performance of firms when they compete for jobs in the construction industry.

CONCLUSION

The study clarifies the different types of successful strategies adopted by firms in the construction industry. In this context, it is noted that firms in an industry with a myriad of strategies can co-exist more easily than in one where all or a majority of the firms are aligned to the same strategy. These strategies were identified based on a review of the construction market with respect to Porter's (1998, 2004) five competitive forces. To ensure profitability, construction firms need to strengthen their implementation ability, even if they are pursuing the same strategy. Thus, even with a better knowledge of the nature and structure of the construction industry, the success of firms can vary in the long run because they may differ in their abilities to implement the same common strategy.

The study also found that construction firms are better off in making a reasonable profit if they have participated in joint ventures with more competent construction-related firms, rather than acting on their own self-interests as their strategic position. By avoiding aggressive price retaliation in the industry, construction firms can focus better on improving their performance and in rendering the whole construction industry better off in terms of profitability and growth. Hence, this can help to elevate the performance of the construction industry to even greater heights.

RECOMMENDATIONS FOR FUTURE WORK

The strategies which the various construction firms have adopted will change with time when different procurement systems start to surface in the industry. Hence, similar studies should be followed through periodically every five to ten years to account for these changes in procurement systems. The study can be further extended to a larger sample size by including all the construction firms in a particular country for it to better reflect the strategic position of the construction industry as a whole.

APPENDIX 1. INTERVIEW QUESTIONNAIRE

RESEARCH ON THE DIFFERENT STRATEGIES USED BY CONSTRUCTION FIRMS IN SINGAPORE

We are conducting a study to determine the different strategies adopted by construction firms in Singapore and to explore the underlying factors that contribute to their competitive advantage.

We would like to assure you that the findings are purely for research purpose only. Hence your identity and that of your organization will remain anonymous.

Section A.

General Information

a) Name of company: _____

Name of respondent: _____

Designation:_____

Years of experience in the construction industry:_____

b) Main business of the company in Singapore: _____

Section B

Interview Questions

1. What do you think of the outlook of the economy and is your prediction of the current economy as what you have expected?
    a. What is the aim of your company during this time of economic boom as well as in the future?
    b. How has the position of your company changed during such times?
2. What are the project financing arrangements for your current projects? How did your company reduce loss due to rising interest rate on loans?
3. In the event of sand ban/local conditions/glut in the global construction industry, how did your company attempt to rectify the situation to ensure you still have a healthy profit margin? Moreover, how do you ensure that you are able to procure the materials at a favorable price to you?
    a. How has the current environment affected your contractual agreement with your client/developer?
    b. Although the most direct impact is from the sudden sand ban imposed by the Indonesian government, there are cumulative damaging effects on other aspects as well. Have the alternatives to sand also become expensive?
4. With rising prices and competitive tenders, what are some of your tendering strategies to ensure that you remain competitive (Cost based/Market based)?
5. Did your company encounter delay due to subcontractors' or suppliers' default? What were the impacts? What measures did your company take to mitigate the loss? How did your company prevent the employment of such subcontractors and suppliers?
6. What are some of the cost saving construction and project management methods which you have employed that had helped you tremendously?
7. Do you think your company has an advantage over costs or differentiation? If others, Please specify.
    a. Please state how did your company achieve this?
8. Please briefly describe the technological or business changes or improvements which your company has planned for during the next couple of years. Is there a shift to cut costs from the product itself, i.e. increase in productivity etc? Do you see yourself investing more towards developing critical technologies to increase your operational effectiveness?

9. Were there any unsuccessful strategies? What are the new obstacles to innovation?

   a.   What do you think the future obstacles are for you?

10. What do you think of the current role of the government? Any possible recommendations or roles do you think the government can undertake to improve the local construction sector?

End of interview. Thank you for your time.

REFERENCES

Acar, E., Kocak, I. Sey, Y. and Arditi, D. (2005) Use of information and communication technologies by small and medium-sized enterprises (SMEs) in building construction. *Construction Management and Economics* 23(7):713-722.

Allen, R. S. and Helms, M. M. (2006) Linking strategic principles and organizational performance to Porter's generic strategies. *Business Process Management Journal* 12(4):433-454.

Ashworth, A. and Skitmore, R. M. (1983) Accuracy in estimating. *The Chartered Institute of Building Occasional Paper Series,* Paper No. 27, 14pp.

Bajari, P. and Ye, L. (2003) Deciding between competition and collusion. *The Review of Economics and Statistics* 85(4):971-989.

Beinhocker, E. D. (1997) Strategy at the edge of chaos. *Mckinsey Quarterly* 199 (1):25-39.

Bennett, J. and Jayes, S. L. (1995) *Trusting the Team: The Best Practice Guide to Partnering in Construction.* Thomas Telford, London.

Best, R. and de Valence, G. (eds.) (1999) *Building in value: pre-design issues.* Arnold, London.

Chan, K. W. and Mauborgne, R. (1999) Creating new market space. *Harvard Business Review* 77:83-93.

Cheah, C. Y. J, and Garvin, M. J. (2004) An open framework for corporate strategy in construction. *Engineering, Construction and Architectural Management* 11(3):176-188.

Cheam, J. (2007) Contractors hit by sand ban to get help. *The Straits Times,* Singapore, 12 May 2007, p.12.

Chen, S. H. (1985) *Effects of Recession on the Construction Industry*, unpublished BSc (Building) Dissertation, School of Building and Estate Management, National University of Singapore.

Committee for Economic Development (1954) *Defense against Recession: Policy for Greater Economic Stability,* A Statement on National Policy by the Research and Policy Committee of the Committee for Economic Development, New York.

Construction 21 Steering Committee (1999) *Re-inventing construction.* Ministry of Manpower and Ministry of National Development, Singapore.

Cordova, E. and Dror, D. (1984) *Collective Bargaining: A Response to the Recession in Industrialised Market Countries,* International Labour Office, Geneva.

Crowley, L. G. and Hancher, D. E. (1995) Evaluation of competitive bids. *Journal of Construction Engineering and Management* 121(2):238-45.

Danson, M. (ed.) (1986) *Redundancy and Recession: Restructuring the Regions,* GeoBooks, Norwich, England.

Dulaimi, M. F., Ling, F. Y. Y., Ofori, G. and De Silva, N. (2002) Enhancing integration and innovation in construction. *Building Research and Information* 30(4):237-247.

Feurer, R. and Chaharbaghi, K. (1997) Strategy development: past, present and future, *Training for Quality* 5(2):58-70.

Gann, D. M. (1996) Construction as a manufacturing process? Similarities and differences between industrialized housing and car production in Japan. *Construction Management and Economics* 14(3):437-450.

Gann, D. M. and Salter, A. (2000) Innovation in project-based, service-enhanced firms: The construction of complex products and systems. *Research Policy* 29:955-972.

Ghemawat, P. (1985) Building strategy on the experience curve. *Harvard Business Review* 63:143-49.

Hambrick, D. C. (1983) High profit strategies in mature capital goods industries: A contingency approach. *Academy of Management Journal* 26(4):687-707.

Helms, M. M., Clay, D. and Peter, W. (1997) Competitive strategies and business performance evidence from the adhesives and sealants industry. *Management Decision* 35(9):689-703.

Hill, C. W. L. (1988) Differentiation versus low cost of differentiation and low cost: a contingency framework. *Academy of Management Review* 13(3):401-412.

Hlavacka, S., Bacharova, L., Rusnakova, V. and Wagner, R. (2001) Performance implications of Porter's generic strategies in Slovak hospitals. *Journal of Management in Medicine* 15 (1):44-66.

Honer, M. and Zakieh R. (1996) Characteristics items – a new approach to pricing and controlling construction projects. *Construction Management and Economics* 14(1):214-252.

Hsieh, H. H. Y. (2005) The 1990s Taiwan residential construction boom; a supply side interpretation. *Construction Management and Economics* 23(1):265-284.

Jackson, C. (1989) Building a competitive advantage through information technology. *Long Range Planning* 22(4):29-39.

Johnson, J., and Scholes, K. (1999) Exploring Corporate Strategy, Texts and Cases, 5th Ed., Prentice Hall: London.

Kim, S. (1997) Organization and managerial environment of the Korean construction industry. *Construction Management and Economics* 15(2):409-419.

King, S. S. and Cushman, D. P. (eds.) (1997) *Lessons from the Recession: A Management and Communication Perspective*, State University of New York Press.

Knuf, J. (2000) Benchmarking the lean enterprise: organizational learning at work. *Journal of Management in Engineering* 16(4):58-71.

Koskela, L. (1992) *Application of the new production philosophy to the construction industry*. CIFE Technical Report No.72, Centre for Integrated Facility Engineering, Stanford University.

Kozminski, A. K. (1997) Lessons from recession in Central and Eastern Europe: from survival to continuous improvement, in King, S. S. and Cushman, D. P. (eds.), *Lessons from the Recession: A Management and Communication Perspective*, State University of New York Press, pp.151-178.

Lo, W., Lin, C. L. and Yan, M. R. (2007) Contractor's opportunistic bidding behavior and equilibrium price level in the construction market. *Journal of Construction Engineering and Management* 133(2):409-416.

Low, S. P. (1992) The strategic outlook for construction business. *Construction Economics Report,* 3rd Quarter, Construction Industry Development Board, Singapore, pp.1-13.

Low, S. P. (1996) *Theory and practice of construction export marketing.* Avebury, Aldershot, United Kingdom.

Low, S. P. and Abdul Aziz, A. R. (1993) *Competitive strategies for the global construction industry.* Trade Link Media, Singapore.

Low, S. P. and Chan, Y. M. (1999) *Managing productivity in construction. JIT operations and measurements.* Ashgate, Aldershot, United Kingom.

Low, S. P. and Leong, C. H. Y. (2001) Asian management style versus western management theories: A Singapore case study in construction project management. *Journal of Managerial Psychology* 16(2):127-141.

Low, S. P. and Lim, N. H. (1999) The strategic responses of construction firms to the Asian financial crisis in 1997-1998. *International Journal of Construction Marketing* 1(2):1-12.

Low, S. P. and Teo, H. F. (2005) Modern-day lean construction principles: Some questions on their origin and similarities with Sun Tzu's Art of War. *Management Decision* 43(4):523-541.

Low, S. S. (1992) Business Strategies of Singapore Contractors, *SES Journal*, 20(6), pp. 16-21.

Macomber, J. D. (1989) You can manage construction risks. *Harvard Business Review* 67(2):155-161.

Mahmoud-Jouini, S. B. (2000) Innovative supply-based strategies in the construction industry. *Construction Management and Economics* 18(6):643-650.

McNamee, P. and Mchugh, M. (1989) Competitive strategies in the clothing industry. *Long Range Planning* 22(4):63-71.

Miller, D. (1992) The generic strategy trap. *Journal of Business Strategy* 13(1):37-42.

Miller, A. and Dess, G. (1993) Assessing Porter's (1980) model in terms of its generalizability, accuracy and simplicity. *Journal of Management Studies* 30(4):37-42.

Ming, C. S., Runeson, G. and Skitmore M. (1996) Changes in profit as market conditions change: An historical study of a building firm. *Construction Management and Economics* 14(3):253-264.

Mochtar, K. and Arditi, D. (2001) Pricing strategy in the US construction industry. *Construction Management and Economics* 19(2):405-415.

Montresor, S. (2001) Resource, capabilities, competences and the theory of the firm. *Journal of Economic Studies* 30(5):409-421.

Morine, F.J. (1980) *Riding the Recession: How to Cope with Shrinking Markets and High Inflation,* Business Books, London.

Ng, D. (2007) Higher prices will force builders to get creative. *The New Paper,* Singapore, 20th March, p.21.

Ngowi, A. B., Iwisi, D. S. and Mushi, R. J. (2002) Competitive strategy in a context of low financial resources. *Building Research and Information* 30(3):205-211.

Nueno, P. (ed.) (1993) *Corporate Turnaround: A Practical Guide to Business Survival,* Kogan Page, New Jersey.

Ofori, G. (2002) Singapore's construction: moving toward a knowledge-based industry. *Building Research and Information* 30(6):401-412.

Palmer, G. (1991) *Surviving the Recession: Practical Ways to Cope with Tough times and Prepare for Renewal,* Business International Ltd., United Kingdom.

Penrose, E. (ed.) (1995) *The Theory of the Growth of the Firm,* Oxford University Press.

Porter, M. (1981) The contributions of industrial organization to strategic management. *Academy of Management Review* 6(4):609-620.

Porter, M. (1996) What is strategy? *Harvard Business Review* 74(6):61-78.

Porter, M. (1998) *Competitive strategy: techniques for analyzing industries and competitors.* The Free Press, New York.

Porter, M. (2004) *Competitive advantage: creating and sustaining superior performance.* The Free Press, New York.

Prescott, J. (1982) *How to Survive the Recession: A Guide to Basic Business Controls Designed to Ensure Your Business will Survive the Recession,* Financial Training Publications Ltd., United Kingdom.

Raftery, J. et al (1998) Globalization and construction industry development: implications of recent developments in the construction sector in Asia. *Construction Management and Economics* 16(5):729-737.

Rahman, M. M. and Kumaraswamy, M. M. (2004) Contracting relationship trends and transitions. *Journal of Management in Engineering* 20(4):147–161.

Robert, G. D. and O'Brien, F. A. (1998) *Strategic development: Methods and Models.* John Wiley and Sons Ltd, New York.

Rugman, A. and Verbeke, A. (1996) Global competition: beyond the three generics. *Research in Global Strategic Management* 36(1):85-89.

Rwelamila, P. D. (2002) Creating an effective industry strategy construction in South Africa. *Building Research and Information* 30(6):435-445.

Sacks, R. and Harel, M. (2006) An economic game theory model of subcontractor resource allocation behavior *Construction Management and Economics* 24(8):869-881.

Seaden, G., et al (2003) Strategic decisions and innovation in construction firms. *Construction Management and Economics* 21(6):603-612.

Serpell, A. and Ocaranza, R. (2001) Technology innovation in the Chilean construction industry: a diagnosis of the current Situation. *International Conference on Innovation in Architecture, Engineering and Construction (AEC),* 18-20 July, Loughbourough, United Kingdom, pp.299-308.

Sexton, M., Barrett, P. and Aouad, G. (2006) Motivating small construction companies to adapt new technology. *Building Research and Information* 34(2):11-22.

Shilling, A. G. (1988) *After the Crash: Recession or Depression? Business and Investment Strategies for a Deflationary World*, Lakeview Economic Services, Short Hills, New Jersey.

Slatter, S. (1992) *Gambling on Growth: How to Manage the Small High-tech Firm*, John Wiley & Sons.

Smith, T. M., James, S. and Reece, J. S. (1999) The relationship of strategy, fit, productivity, and business performance in a services setting *Journal of Operations Management* 17(2):145-161.

Spanos, Y. E., Zaralis, G. and Lioukas, S. (2004) Strategy and industry effects on profitability: evidence from Greece. *Strategic Management Journal* 25(1):139-165.

Stephen, L. G. and Graham, J. L (2000) *The economics of the modern construction firm*. Macmillan Press Ltd, London.

Tingle, L. (1994) *Chasing the Future: Recession, Recovery and the New Politics in Australia*, William Heinemann, Australia.

Townsend, A. R. (1983) *The Impact of Recession: On Industry, Employment and the Region, 1976-1981*, Croom Helm, London.

Whiltington, R. (1989) *Corporate Strategies in Recession and Recovery: Social Structure and Strategic Choice*, Unwin Hyman, London.

Whitla, P., Walters, P. and Davies, H. (2006) The use of global strategies by British construction firms. *Construction Management and Economics* 24(9):945-954.

Wright, R. E. (1996) A refinement of Porter's strategies. *Strategic Management Journal* 7(2):217-231.

Wright, P., et al (1991) Generic strategies and business performance: an empirical study of the screw machine products industry. *British Journal of Management* 2 (1):57-65.

INDEX